Financial Ethics

Financial Ethics
A Positivist Analysis

GEORGE A. ARAGON

OXFORD
UNIVERSITY PRESS

2011

OXFORD
UNIVERSITY PRESS

Oxford University Press, Inc., publishes works that further
Oxford University's objective of excellence
in research, scholarship, and education.

Oxford New York
Auckland   Cape Town   Dar es Salaam   Hong Kong   Karachi
Kuala Lumpur   Madrid   Melbourne   Mexico City   Nairobi
New Delhi   Shanghai   Taipei   Toronto

With offices in
Argentina   Austria   Brazil   Chile   Czech Republic   France   Greece
Guatemala   Hungary   Italy   Japan   Poland   Portugal   Singapore
South Korea   Switzerland   Thailand   Turkey   Ukraine   Vietnam

Published by Oxford University Press, Inc.
198 Madison Avenue, New York, New York 10016

www.oup.com

Oxford is a registered trademark of Oxford University Press

Library of Congress Cataloging-in-Publication Data
Aragon, George A.
Financial ethics: a positivist analysis / by George A. Aragon.
p. cm.
Includes bibliographical references and index.
ISBN 978-0-19-530596-8
1. Finance—Moral and ethical aspects. I. Title.
HG173.A793 2010
174'.4—dc22   2010004232

9 8 7 6 5 4 3 2 1

Printed in the United States of America
on acid-free paper

Preface

The target audience for this book is finance academics who are interested in exploring the connections between ethics and finance. We call the scope of all of these connections "financial ethics." The interested reader may be pleasantly surprised to find that these connections are not only pervasive but also that they continue to emerge in more explicit fashion in mainstream financial research.

To argue that the connections between ethics and finance are likely to be substantial, one need only consider the long, multifaceted relationship between economics and ethics. From its origins in moral philosophy through its struggle to develop into an independent social science, economics has had an intimate, often conflicted, relationship with ethics. This relationship continues to be viewed as relevant as indicated in the work of many eminent economists including several Nobel laureates (e.g., Gary Becker, Amartya Sen, Kenneth Arrow, James Buchanan, George Akerlof, and Joseph Stiglitz).

For its part, over the last half-century finance has developed away from management science into a subfield of economics, incorporating the canonical assumptions of economics (i.e., self-interest, rationality, and equilibrium), its methodological approach (positivism), and its techniques (e.g., mathematics, econometrics, game theory). This process of integration has become so complete that, as Gibbons (1987) observes, most finance researchers consider themselves to be "financial economists."

While the reader may prefer to distinguish between the ethical concerns of economics and the ethical concerns of finance, this distinction has become increasingly irrelevant. Thus, the concepts of moral hazard and adverse selection developed in economics, both of which contain important ethical dimensions, have found wide application in many areas of finance (e.g., agency cost theory and signaling theory).

In our view, the scope of financial ethics is vast. To make the study of this area more manageable, we somewhat arbitrarily split the field into two distinct though clearly related frameworks. We will define "normative financial ethics" as the application of moral concepts to evaluate and prescribe the conduct of economic agents. It is probably the case that most academics view financial ethics only in this dimension as evidenced by

the voluminous amount of research devoted to it by none-finance scholars (such as business ethicists), but, as we will argue later, also by the vigorous opposition to the very notion of financial ethics by many financial economists. Clearly, normative financial ethics requires moral argumentation and an understanding of alternative moral systems. For reasons explained in chapter 1, research that adopts this normative approach to finance is omitted from our study.

In contrast to normative financial ethics, "positive financial ethics" is concerned only with describing, explaining, and predicting the economic consequences of moral behavior. More precisely, we consider the impact of expected moral behavior on the process of exchange and, ultimately, the determination of economic value. Although the result of such an analysis naturally leads to normative considerations, we leave this extension outside the scope of our study. Put simplistically, in the language of financial economics, it is useful to think of positive financial ethics as a study of the question "Are ethical expectations priced in transactions?"

We address this question by examining both theoretical and empirical financial economics research. Undoubtedly, many academics will question the possibility of a positive financial ethics. Yet, we will contend that moral preconceptions, or expectations, do affect economic value. The classic example of just such a case is that of Akerlof's (1970) "lemons" model in which information asymmetries may lead to market failure when agents are expected to be dishonest. The dual conditions for market failure; that is, information asymmetries and dishonesty, suggested by Akerlof's model, reflect the key link between economic value and ethics. In particular, we will argue that information asymmetries are necessary but not sufficient to produce market failure; it is also necessary that some assumption about the moral character of agents be introduced. Importantly, we assume that agents have probability distributions around the moral character of others and that the means of these distributions vary from context to context and from agent to agent. As these expectations vary, so do underlying economic values.

Befitting our perspective, we pursue a positivist methodology to examine whether and how ethical expectations influence economic value. This methodology relies exclusively on mainstream financial economics. Classifying research in this way may encourage and enable interested finance academics to consider these and other connections, because it not only avoids the normative elements but also because it is based on research and assumptions that are familiar to financial economists.

In our framework for positive financial ethics we avoid debates over what is meant by "morality" or by "economic rationality." These debates are endless and well beyond the scope of this study. Instead, we use "rough and ready conceptions." For example, by economic rationality we mean, essentially, the pursuit of narrow self-interest; by morality we mean philosophical systems such as deontology, utilitarianism, virtue, and justice that provide a basis to guide human behavior. Moreover, unless specific distinctions are made, we use the terms "economics," "finance," and "financial economics" interchangeably. Likewise, we use the terms "moral" and "ethical" interchangeably.

Perhaps needless to say, we do not attempt original research in the field of positive financial ethics. Our modest objective is to simply organize existing mainstream financial research in a way that highlights the many connections between finance and ethics. Classifying research in this way may encourage and enable interested finance academics to consider this connection. In addition, any credible positivist analysis of the proposition that finance is "value-free" would have to be firmly grounded in mainstream financial economics research; otherwise some readers would dismiss it as rhetoric.

Our organizing paradigm for positive financial ethics is the process of exchange. For clarity, we assume this process takes place between two economic agents in a nonmarket transaction.

Loosely, we examine three broad settings for this exchange. First, we examine the situation where there is an asymmetric power relationship (including both informational advantages and monopoly power) between the two agents such that the stronger agent may expropriate value from the weaker (i.e., less informed or dependent) agent. Broadly speaking, this action, whether legal or illegal, corresponds to our notion of "theft." Second, regardless whether the power relationship is symmetric or not, one agent may voluntarily and wittingly transfer value to the counterparty. This action corresponds to our notion of "altruism." Third, and related to the altruism setting, we consider a situation in which one agent (the "trustor") voluntarily and knowingly exposes himself to theft by the "trustee" in hopes of productive cooperation. In contrast to altruism, the trustor does not intend to transfer value but rather to enable mutually rewarding cooperative behavior. This notion corresponds to our definition of trust.

The notions of theft, altruism, and trust naturally encompass many related ideas. For example, theft encompasses agency costs, free riding, and expropriation. Altruism incorporates the notions of fairness and justice, among other things; while trust also incorporates the notion of fairness.

The approach to financial ethics adopted in this book will undoubtedly be provocative or even disappointing to some; and, thus, it is necessary to state at the outset what this book is about and what it is not about.

This book is not about detailing the recent scandals of financial practice or formally examining the moral validity of narrowly itself-interested agents; nor is this book intended to provide guidance for making ethically defensible financial decisions or to argue that there should be "more ethics" in finance. These are all worthy objectives for a book dealing with finance and ethics and they have been pursued by many respected scholars; particularly in the field of business ethics. Unfortunately, these contributions have typically enjoyed limited success among finance academics in both research and teaching; and finance academics have been conspicuously absent in their contributions to the field of financial ethics.

The reasons for such resistance are very likely numerous and we discuss some of them in more detail in the next chapter.

But clearly one of the most salient factors must be that financial economists, mistakenly, in my opinion, view the discipline as "scientific," "technical," or "value-free." We will argue later that this view is fundamentally flawed since even the narrowest conception of economic man (i.e., exclusively self-interested) has an explicit moral premise, that is, egoism. Moreover, the resistance to financial ethics impedes the contributions of financial economics to the resolution of important social problems, such as those of corporate governance and the adverse consequences of poorly designed regulations.

For many financial economists, the discomfort with ethical concepts is resolved by treating all such concepts as part of the ceteris paribus conditions, essentially exogenous to the financial decisions or behaviors analyzed (i.e., the agent's preferences are taken as given). Yet, there is bound to be endogeneity between the financial decision and ethical behavior. Such an assumption of endogeneity is in fact crucial to the design of incentive systems designed to alter agent behavior; but without a proper understanding of this endogeneity ex ante, the consequences of incentive systems may be completely perverse to what was expected. One need only cite the perverse incentives to lie and cheat created by performance-based compensation plans or the subversion of the net present value rule by self-interested managers who are more concerned with short-term reputation effects than long-term shareholder value.

Alternatively, other financial economists acknowledge the fact that individuals are interested in things other than monetary gain (e.g., integrity and altruism), but because money is fungible, such agents are able to trade off monetary for nonmonetary goods. In this view, there is a presumption that maximizing monetary gain is a close "first approximation" to satisfying the agent's monetary and nonmonetary preferences.

Hence, nonmonetary goods, such as ethical goods, can be treated as of second–order importance. Again, without a better understanding of the relationship between monetary and nonmonetary goods in the agent's utility function, unintended consequences can result. For example, in some cases monetary rewards may crowd out voluntary altruistic behaviors. In other cases, relationships between, for example, principals and agents may be radically altered by impersonal reward systems.

The framework just described does seem to create an impasse and, if correct, helps explain the resistance that financial economists have to introducing ethics into their research and teaching.

For such reasons alone, this book strikes a different path from other works on financial ethics. First, and most important, our framework recognizes that there are actually two fundamental challenges incorporated in the impasse posed above: 1) to demonstrate that ethics is relevant to financial analysis because it is a factor affecting valuation in exchange; and 2) that because of 1), financial economists should be motivated to invest effort in developing a better understanding of how economic value may be enhanced by ethical behavior. These two challenges fall, roughly, into two broad categories. The first challenge is an empirical question and can be addressed by what may be loosely characterized as "positive theory," while the second challenge loosely conforms to what may be called "normative theory." This distinction implies two broad dimensions to financial ethics, namely, positive financial ethics and normative financial ethics.

To illustrate the distinction we are trying to draw between the two dimensions of financial ethics, consider its analog in conventional capital market research. Risk is considered important in financial analysis because it has been shown that it affects value (this is the challenge of item [1] above). And, because risk does affect economic value, financial decisions are enriched by a better understanding of risk in its many varieties (this is the challenge of item [2]). Without first having established the relevance of risk to finance it would be difficult to attract the interest or attention of financial economists. Similarly with financial ethics. Our proposition is that progress toward incorporating normative concerns will proceed much more rapidly once the role of ethics in valuation is shown to be important.

Contents

CHAPTER 1

Normative and Positive Approaches to Financial Ethics

1.1 A WORKING DEFINITION OF FINANCIAL ETHICS

The variety of interrelationships between finance and ethics goes under many different names such as "ethics and finance," "finance ethics," "ethical finance," and "financial ethics." The various designations undoubtedly derive at least in part from the relative emphasis the researcher wants to place on finance or ethics. Nonetheless, while we prefer the term "financial ethics" all of these variations are logically bounded at the intersection of the fields of finance and ethics possessing elements of each. Thus financial ethics is a subfield of ethics and finance.

Moreover, we will argue that this common area can be viewed from the perspective of either finance or ethics, and that the particular approach adopted is a major determinant of the type of questions examined and methodologies employed. For example, a strictly financial perspective begins with the question, are moral behaviors such as honesty rewarded? This question can be examined both theoretically and empirically.

In contrast, from an ethical perspective an analogous research question would be something like, is insider trading morally defensible? In order to answer this type of question, various theories of moral argumentation are drawn upon. Put simplistically, the financial dimension of financial ethics takes moral behaviors as givens[1] and examines their economic consequences while the ethical dimension takes financial choices as given and examines their moral status.

The interplay of these various concepts enriches the scope of financial ethics in limitless directions. Thus financial ethics may involve, from an ethical framework, the examination of such diverse issues as the fiduciary duties of managers to shareholders; the responsibility corporations have to stakeholders and society at large; to considerations of whether insider trading is moral; and whether economic agents should, if given the chance, expropriate value from others. Alternatively, from a financial perspective, financial ethics involves an objective examination of the effects of, for example, honesty on valuation, trust on efficiency, and self-interest on altruism.

In the process of examining such questions and generalizing from them, new and perhaps unexpected research areas are revealed, further expanding the field. One classic example of this is that of the effects of dishonesty and information asymmetries on the operation of markets (Akerlof 1970). A study of the resulting adverse selection problem not only

---

1. This does raise the obvious but difficult issue of identifying moral and immoral behaviors. Rather, at this preliminary stage, and particularly given the focus of this book, we avoid trying to define the "true" meaning of the terms. Instead, we simply adopt the commonsense interpretations of moral behavior; i.e., including notions of honesty, fairness, trust, altruism, and justice. We should also note here that there is an inescapable entangling of the two perspectives; i.e., financial and ethical, since, if certain moral behaviors correlate with superior outcomes, rational economic actors will find it in their best self-interest to pursue them.

reveals a vast scope of applications relevant to finance but also invites an exploration into the formal and informal mechanisms, such as contract and reputation, that address it. Simultaneously, from an ethical perspective the issue of adverse selection also permits the examination as to whether the externalities created from such opportunistic activity (i.e., the pursuit of narrow self-interest) in such circumstances is morally justifiable.

It is apparent from the preceding examples that the field of financial ethics lends itself to a natural partition of interrelationships that can be categorized, on the one hand, as normative (e.g., whether insider trading is moral), and on the other hand, as positivist (e.g., what is the effect of insider trading on market efficiency?). We employ this partition to identify two interrelated subfields of financial ethics: "normative" financial ethics (NFE) and "positive" financial ethics (PFE). In order to make these concepts manageable, we adopt the conventional meaning of the terms "normative" and "positive." We assume that NFE involves evaluative and prescriptive "ought" statements, while PFE involves descriptive, explanatory, and predictive "cause-and-effect" statements. The methodologies of the two subfields also differ significantly. Normative financial ethics typically relies on the methodology of moral argumentation while PFE relies on the methodology of positivist science (e.g., description, theory, hypothesis-building, explanation, prediction, and testing).

In the next section, we will examine why researchers in financial ethics have been almost exclusively preoccupied with the normative interpretation. We will argue that as a result, contributions to the field had been made overwhelmingly by nonfinancial economists and explore why financial economists, who take pride in keeping their discipline "value-free," have almost universally rejected financial ethics as a serious field of research.

1.2   FINANCIAL ETHICS AND BUSINESS ETHICS

Most financial economists probably consider financial ethics to be little more than a subfield of business ethics. While plausible enough since finance is a subdiscipline of business, this association can lead to a serious limitation of the scope and relevance of financial ethics to financial economists. To see how this can happen, it is important to review the development of business ethics as an academic field.

In his overview of the history of business ethics, Richard De George (2005) identifies three important strands: (1) an "ethics in business" strand; (2) the development of business ethics as an academic field strand; and (3) the strand as a cultural movement used to explicitly build ethics into the structures of corporations in the form of ethics codes, ethics officers, ethics committees, and ethics training. We will discuss only the first two of these strands since they are most germane to this book.

The "ethics in business" strand can be traced as far back as business itself and is characterized by its emphasis on business abuses, particularly financial scandals. De George notes:

> This strand of the story is perhaps the most prominent in the thinking of the ordinary person when they hear the term *business ethics*. The media carries stories about Enron officials acting unethically and about the unethical activities of Arthur Andersen or WorldCom, and so on, and the general public takes this as representative of business ethics or of the need for it. *What they mean is the need for ethics in business* (page number, emphasis added).

Likewise, in finance, it is not unusual to hear the term "financial ethics" also equated with financial scandals and condemned as immoral by the media as well as moral authorities and professors of business. In this light it is not surprising that most financial economists dismiss financial ethics as nothing more than moralizing or preaching; it simply lacks intellectual rigor.

Unfortunately, even in its academic setting business ethics, according to De George, began with, primarily, a concern for issues such as the social responsibility of business and issues in management activities, such as discrimination. Although early academic research in this strand consisted of a handful of courses with the name "business ethics and empirical research" (such as case studies), ethical issues, if they were discussed, "were handled in social issues courses." Yet these efforts did not culminate in a formal academic field because, according to De George, until the 1970s they lacked a theoretical framework for identifying and evaluating the ethical quality of behavior at the individual, organizational, and systemic levels. De George observes:

> The new ingredient and the catalyst that led to the field of business ethics as such was the entry of a significant number of philosophers, who brought ethical theory and philosophical analysis to bear on a variety of issues in business. Business ethics emerged as a result of the intersection of ethical theory with empirical studies and the analysis of cases and issues. (2005, 11)

This catalyst brought with it a particular approach—one relying on ethical theory at its base. According to De George, "Discussions of business ethics introduced students to…the basic techniques of moral argumentation" (11). Many different techniques could be applied to what may be called business issues or dilemmas. For example, deontological theories emphasize moral duties such as those of agents to principals and vice versa. Virtue theories emphasize the importance of character and excellence in conduct. Consequentialist or utilitarian theories focus on the balance between beneficial and harmful effects of alternative decisions. Justice theories invoke concepts of fairness and equity. Thus the same decision problem can be approached from many different ethical perspectives, and perhaps not surprisingly, can yield different choices. For example, the principal-agent problem can be evaluated both from the perspective of the duty of managers to owners, but also from a consequentialist perspective (i.e., whether blind adherence to such duties will cause more harm than good). Yet the common purpose of all these forms of moral argumentation, as noted by De George, has been to identify, evaluate, and prescribe the quality of ethical behavior in business.

Thus whether from its "ethics in business" dimension or its academic dimension, the distinctive character of business ethics has been normative. As a result, equating financial ethics with business ethics (as it has developed) confines financial ethics to a normative framework. It is not surprising, then, that financial economists avoid or reject financial ethics as being outside the discipline.

As noted, the term "financial ethics" is typically viewed as purely normative. This raises the question as to whether there is or can be such a thing as positive financial ethics. It may be useful to think of positive financial ethics the way one thinks of positive financial economics. Like positive financial economics, positive financial ethics attempts to describe, explain, and predict economic institutions and behaviors. But positive financial ethics is distinctive in that it focuses on the financial effects of ethical behavior[2] such as honesty, fairness, altruism, and trust. As a positive theory, positive financial ethics emphasizes cause-and-effect relationships and the use of abstractions to model and test the predicted economic consequences of ethical and unethical behavior. Positive financial ethics addresses questions such as, what are the effects of dishonesty on firm value? In this model, moral

2. More specifically, "expected" ethical behavior; discussed in chapter 2.

argumentation is not directly involved; ethical behaviors are taken as given and their financial consequences are examined. Inevitably, of course, such analyses will lead to normative prescriptions, since rational economic agents will choose the optimal course of action.

In short, the distinction we are attempting to draw between NFE and PFE follows the suggestion by Daniel Hausman and Michael McPherson that one way to bring moral notions into economics is to empirically examine the influence of moral norms on people's behavior:

> This approach starts from the apparent fact that people's economic behavior is influenced by their moral beliefs, and it looks to see what impact these beliefs have on economic outcomes. At least to begin with, one can pursue this approach in a purely "positive" light—asking not whether these moral beliefs are justified, but simply whether they are behaviorally effective. Rather quickly, however, such work turns to the question of whether the observed moral commitments are economically beneficial or pernicious, and at that point the normative and positive dimensions intertwine. Work on these lines tends to use rough and ready conceptions of economic rationality and of morality—the aim is to find categories that help sort out empirical phenomena. (1993, 679)

For our purposes we adopt general methodologies suggested by Hausman and McPherson; that is, we begin with an analysis of positive financial ethics and how it relates to normative financial ethics; second, we then follow with a study of the key elements of a theory of positive financial ethics; third, we examine the empirical evidence as it relates to these key elements; and finally, we discover how the positive and normative of financial ethics dimensions can be reconciled on the basis of empirical results. The next section describes the sequence we follow in developing this manuscript.

1.3   ORGANIZATION OF THE BOOK

In chapter 2 we attempt to provide an introductory outline of the scope and methods of financial ethics. We will argue the field comprises two distinct though interrelated dimensions; namely, a normative dimension and a positivist dimension. Although this book is concerned with the latter, we will, nonetheless, briefly describe what may be meant by normative financial ethics and how this contrasts with positive financial ethics.

Chapter 3 discusses the connection between ethics and valuation. Key to this connection are the ethical expectations among interacting agents, which we define as the a priori assessments of the ethical behavior of counterparties in a particular exchange relationship. A distinction is drawn between "ethics-like" behavior and ethical behavior driven by intrinsic moral character. We argue that although there is a clear and important relationship between the intrinsic moral character of agents and expectations as to their behavior, it is only the expected behavior itself that is of first-order importance to positive financial ethics. More concretely, even intrinsically immoral agents may behave "as-if" they were ethical, if properly incented. This concept of "as-if-ness" is consistent with model building in positive economics.

Finally, we distinguish between expropriation risk and ethical risk, whereby, expropriation risk represents the potential expropriation of one party by another while ethical risk represents the expected expropriation (i.e., the product of ethical expectations and potential expropriation). It is ethical risk, that is, expected expropriation, that affects economic value in exchange. Lacking safeguards, financial economics typically assumes that any expropriation opportunity will be fully exploited by economically rational agents and hence expropriation risk and ethical risk are equivalent. However, where safeguards are present, there may be a considerable divergence between expropriation risk and ethical risk. Consequently, valuation varies with ethical risk.

Chapter 4 focuses directly on the use of safeguards that are designed to promote ethical expectations. Broadly viewed, we term these mechanisms "financial ethical technologies." They are financial technologies because they heighten economic value and they are ethical technologies because their value-enhancing contributions are made by ensuring ethics-like behavior. The variety of such technologies is virtually infinite. Moreover, the variety of such technologies, we argue, arises because of the many different contexts in which transactions (contractual arrangements) occur, as well as the broad variety of the transactions themselves. Moreover, since ethical expectations vary in degree among economic agents (e.g., with regard to different ethical sensitivities of agents), economic relationships (e.g., with regard to contractual completeness), and characteristics of particular transactions (e.g., with regard to asset specificity), ethical technologies will likewise vary in application and importance in the sense of "discriminating alignments" as articulated by Oliver Williamson (1998) in the context of transaction cost economics.

Thus this chapter includes a partial taxonomy of financial ethical technologies, including differential legal régimes, regulatory and supervisory organizations, social norms and customs, contracts, reputation, organizational form, screening, and the media. Though we do not discuss this in much detail, the reader may be interested to read that we consider something as mundane as a burglar alarm or a surveillance camera to be a financial ethical technology insofar as each of these devices deters expropriation and enhances ethical expectations.

The chapter concludes with a discussion of two distinct difficulties that may arise from the use of financial ethical technologies. First, implementation of a particular technology introduces its own new dimension of expropriation risks. For example, the introduction of regulation in financial markets corrects some market failures but introduces the prospect of government failures, as noted by Edward Kane (2002b) and Daron Acemoglu and Thierry Verdier (2000). Likewise, in corporate finance, performance-based compensation such as stock options induces manipulation of financial information (Kane 2003). In short, we argue that there is a dialectical process inherent in the use of financial ethical technologies and thus the array of such technologies is endless.

A second important difficulty is that extrinsic technologies may crowd out intrinsic motivations. By way of example, contracts may crowd out trust, loyalty, and altruism. If the adoption of ethical technologies is done without sufficient foresight, the results may be counterproductive.

In chapter 5 we discuss mainstream research as it relates to positive financial ethics. First, we discuss ethical risk in the context of the functioning of capital markets. Here the focus is on legal protections and regulatory supervision as ways of mitigating ethical risks. The studies we examine focus primarily on differing legal regimes across countries, the attendant size and relative values of capital markets across countries, and cross-sectional variation in share values attributable to governance mechanisms across firms within countries.

Next, we discuss ethical risk pertinent to corporate finance and the financial ethical technologies employed to safeguard against them. Thus we consider both the ex ante technologies employed to mitigate such ethical risks and the ex post evidence as to their effectiveness. For example, among shareholders a variety of ethical risks can arise. For example, "intra-shareholder" expropriation may occur between insiders and outside shareholders between existing shareholders and new shareholders, controlling shareholders versus minority shareholders, restricted-voting versus superior-voting shareholder classes, and targeted shareholders (i.e., "greenmail") versus nontargeted shareholders. Distinctions are also sometimes made between the interests of "short-term" versus "long-term" investors, and between "institutional" versus "noninstitutional" shareholder groups.

Ethical risks also arise in contracting with nonshareholder parties, that is, nonshareholder stakeholders. For example, ethical risks arise for employees (e.g., pension fund reversions), customers (e.g., fraud, manipulation, and price fixing), and suppliers (e.g., bilateral dependency). Again, we examine ethical technologies such as signaling, bonding, and organizational form.

In the sixth and final chapter we examine trust in the context of ethics and economic anomalies. The purpose is to demonstrate how ethical considerations can describe and predict behavior that is inconsistent with "economic rationality."

CHAPTER 2

Financial Ethics as a Field of Study

2.1 INEVITABLE INTERCONNECTIONS BETWEEN FINANCE AND ETHICS

Objectively considered, the development of financial ethics as a field of study would seem to be inevitable. There are many arguments in support of this view but we will discuss four. First, the integration of finance into a subfield of economics, particularly microeconomics, has led not only to an adoption of the assumptions and methodologies of economics but also to an increased interest in the research agenda of economics. Of course, given its origins in moral philosophy, economics has had an extensive and often conflicted relationship to ethics. Second, the extension of applied economic methodologies and assumptions (what Becker [1992] has called the "economic way of looking at life" and which Hirshleifer [1985] has referred to as "economic imperialism") to other fields, including ethics, has made this interaction more likely. Correspondingly, the study of ethics has also aggressively expanded into other areas, including finance and economics, primarily through the vehicle of applied ethics and, more specifically, business ethics. Third, the persistence of massive financial scandals (e.g., Enron, WorldCom) has highlighted the failure of standard economic assumptions about human behavior (e.g., rational expectations) and market efficiency to explain them. Amid calls for more and stricter regulatory controls, such as the Sarbanes-Oxley Act of 2002, the financial landscape has become dramatically altered, necessitating the development of new theories and explanations (e.g., Kane 1990, 2002b, 2003; Akerlof and Romer 1993). Fourth, the role of nonmonetary determinants of capital flows such as "socially responsible investments" or "ethical investing" cannot be adequately explained by conventional capital market theory. Important empirical questions naturally arise, such as the magnitude of such flows, whether investments in socially responsible funds perform worse than investments of similar risk, and whether such capital flows affect corporate stock prices favorably (if the corporation is viewed as socially responsible) or unfavorably (if the corporation is viewed as not being socially responsible). We will discuss each of these factors briefly below.

2.1.1   The Expanding Domains of Economics and Ethics

Jack Hirshleifer (1985) reviews applications of economic methodology to areas well outside economics, what he refers to as "economic imperialism." For example, he notes that the concept of rational self-interest has "invaded" such diverse fields as politics, warfare, mate selection, engineering design, and statistical decisions. Moreover, as with all imperialist enterprises, the invader inevitably incorporates concepts from the vanquished. Hirshleifer argues that even within the domain of market behavior, economics now incorporates such "non-market" factors as cultural, ethical, and even "irrational" forces. He notes:

> While scientific work in anthropology and sociology and political science and the like will become increasingly indistinguishable from economics, economists will reciprocally have to become aware of how constraining has been their tunnel vision about the nature of man and social interactions. Ultimately, good economics will also have to be good anthropology and sociology and political science and psychology. (53)

The expansion of economic methodology to noneconomic areas has required a reformulation of standard agent preference functions to include nonpecuniary motives. For example, in his Nobel lecture, Becker notes:

> To understand discrimination against minorities, it is necessary to widen preferences to accommodate prejudice and hatred of particular groups. The economic analysis of crime incorporates into rational behavior illegal and other antisocial actions. The human capital approach considers how the productivity of people in market and non-market situations is changed by investments in education, skills, and knowledge. The economic approach to the family interprets marriage, divorce, fertility, and relations among family members through the lens of utility-maximizing forward-looking behavior. (1992, 39)

Michael Jensen and William Meckling discuss a model of man that they call the Resourceful, Evaluative, Maximizing Model (or, REMM). In contrast to the narrow economic conception of self-interested agents, REMM allows for preferences other than material goods. For example,

> individuals are willing to sacrifice a little of almost anything we care to name, even reputation or morality, for a sufficiently large

quantity of other desired things, and these things do not have to be money or even material goods.(1994, 7)

For its part, ethics has itself also expanded quickly and significantly into other disciplines including law, medicine, and business through the methodology of applied ethics. The extent to which an ethical perspective has penetrated business management is much too broad to be reviewed in any detail here, but it is worth noting that a great number of business ethics centers, institutes, societies, and associations have been established, either within or directly affiliated with universities. A recent listing of selected business-ethics related resources developed at the Long Business and Economics Library at the Haas School of Business, Berkeley[1] identifies 15 academic journals, 13 Web sites, 5 online encyclopedias, and 225 books and monographs published between 1995 and 2004 devoted to business ethics. Undoubtedly, the actual number of such resources is considerably larger. Ironically, although the field of business ethics has been said to owe its existence to financial scandals, relatively few finance academics have contributed to this field; mainly, as noted by James Ang (1993) and others, because of the lack of incentives for doing such research.

In his positivist analysis of justice in mainstream economics, James Konow argues that the application of justice concepts in economics has not only grown in acceptance but has actually partly displaced studies of efficiency. In his examination of studies documented on *EconLit* he finds:

> The numbers of entries for the 1970s under the keyword "efficiency" outnumber those under "justice" or "fairness" (not counting those under the equivocal term "equity") by sixteen to one. For the 1980s this ratio falls to about nine to one, and for the 1990s this

---

1. See http://www.lib.berkeley.edu/BUSI/ejournals.html for a listing of available journals.

gap further narrows to 4.4 to one. In fact, if one considers entries under the JEL classification system in operation since 1991 through the present, hits under the code closest to justice (D63: Equity, Justice, Inequality, and Other Normative Criteria and Measurement) outnumber those under that closest to efficiency (D61: Allocative Efficiency; Cost-Benefit Analysis) almost two to one. (2003, 1188)

2.1.2   The Evolution of Financial Economic Research

The role of ethics in financial theory has evolved in tandem with the field of financial economics itself. Most dramatically, the impact of imperfect information has endowed economic agents with capacities for behavior that had previously been excluded from neoclassical models of perfectly competitive markets. In these earlier models the focus was on the "black-box" view of finance, as reflected in the net present value criterion in capital budgeting, or either the optimization of investment portfolios relative to risk and return, or the irrelevance of capital structure to the value of the firm. The introduction of market imperfections, particularly information imperfections, opened up a vast new area of financial economics research. The distinctive nature of this new area has been its concern with the risk of theft in its infinite manifestations (e.g., managerial "shirking").

In his review of corporate finance theory over the twenty-five-year period ending in 1995, Michael Brennan identifies important changes in the focus and emphasis of research. According to Brennan,

> The fundamental change has been the recognition of the decisive role of individually motivated agents, both those within the corporation and those with whom the corporation must deal. The corporation of financial theory in the early 1970s ignored individual

agents within the corporation either by assuming that they acted as well-trained robots (as in the investment decision) or by paralyzing them with the ceteris paribus assumptions that underlie the classical capital structure propositions. Similarly, it rendered the individuals with whom the corporation must deal—investors, bankers, underwriters, bidders, customers, employees, and others—essentially uninteresting, by treating them as price takers who suffered from no informational disadvantage and had no relevant aims beyond expanding their budget sets. (1995, 10)

As financial economics has focused increasingly on the economic consequences of imperfect information, such as adverse selection (e.g., the market for "lemons") and moral hazard (e.g., the principal-agent problem), the importance of formal and informal institutions (such as laws, contracts, social norms, organizations) as mechanisms to mitigate the economic costs of such consequences has become increasingly relevant to mainstream research. Nonetheless, financial economists have strongly resisted acknowledging the ethical roots of many such costs. One particularly useful device for circumventing ethical terminology has been the use of neutral-sounding synonyms. One consequence of this is that finance academics effectively insist on leaving all ethical concepts and terminology outside the classroom door and outside of research papers. This type of moral muteness is relentlessly preserved not only in class discussions but also in research and consulting reports. Instead, these concepts are transmuted into less morally charged terminology, for example, by referring to financial manipulation as "income smoothing" lying as "cheap talk," or theft as "rent seeking."

Although semantic revisions may seem innocuous enough, the view taken here is that the important role of ethics in finance is obscured, leading many to maintain that ethics has little if anything to do with finance. However, such attitudes distance finance academics from the common sense of public perception.

Michael Jensen argues:

> Language affects the way the world occurs to people and therefore affects their behavior. When we use terms other than lying to describe earnings management behavior we inadvertently encourage the sacrifice of integrity in corporations and in board rooms and elsewhere. (2006, 19)

This moral muteness is a major obstacle to the introduction of ethics into teaching, research, and consulting by finance academics. In consequence, nonfinance academics, such as ethical theorists, engage in translating the economic characterizations and language used by finance academics back into the ethical meaning of these transmuted concepts. In other words, where finance academics view income smoothing as a substitute for lying, ethical theorists insist on calling it what it is, lying.

To be fair, the burden on financial economists is made much more complex by the fact that there is a broad variety of moral theories and even moral philosophers treat ethical concepts as unresolved. For example, the moral standing of an action may depend upon what moral system is used to evaluate that action. Thus the act of lying or being dishonest may be immoral from the standpoint of duty-based philosophy (i.e., truth telling is a categorical imperative) while morally justifiable from the standpoint of utilitarian philosophy (i.e., if the aggregate benefits from the action exceed the costs).

2.1.3   Financial Scandals

Recent financial scandals have drawn the attention of financial economists to ethics for several reasons. First, the scandals themselves have maligned the discipline and raised questions about what it is that finance academics teach. In response, some financial academics find it necessary to defend the discipline, and increasingly have sought ways to introduce ethics into the finance curriculum. For example, the general knowledge and skills portion of Association to Advance Collegiate Schools of Business (AACSB) standards for undergraduates calls for ethics education in all disciplines. In addition, students themselves may seek support in justifying careers in finance to themselves and others.

Second, the scandals have forced many finance academics to think about their personal moral responsibility for the scope of financial training they provide to students. Students educated in sophisticated financial techniques gain power over the gullible and less informed and thus such knowledge is a weapon that may easily be misused, even if unintentionally. This view is reflected in Warren Buffett's cautionary remarks to shareholders about the potential dangers of derivatives securities, saying, "In our view, derivatives are financial weapons of mass destruction, carrying dangers that, while now latent, are potentially lethal. (2003, 15)" Some academics believe that at least proper warnings as to how powerful financial techniques can produce harm is important.

In an interesting exchange between Brennan (1994) and Jensen (1994) Brennan proposes that the typical characterization of the financial manager as a self-interested maximizer is not only incorrect but potentially damaging. Addressing agency theory in particular, he cautions,

> If we go on hammering into our students the mistaken notion that rationality is identical with self-interest, we shall gradually make our agency models come true, but at the cost of producing a society that will not function. (1994, 39)

Jensen responds that Brennan misconstrues agency theory and its presumption of self-interest. Jensen argues that, for example, the pursuit of self-interest (as in REMM) does not exclude altruism. According to Jensen,

> The satisfaction people get from helping others is another "good" to be sought in their efforts to maximize their own utility. In seeking to achieve the greatest possible good for themselves, people choose from an "opportunity set" that includes love, honor and the welfare of others as well as money and material objects. (1994, 42)

Third, scandals provide a laboratory for financial theory, encouraging financial researchers to explore how massive unethical schemes can be implemented in presumably efficient capital markets or in highly regulated industries. For example, the highly regulated S&L industry motivated financial economists to examine the adverse incentive effects of federal deposit guarantees for reckless risk taking (e.g., Kane 1990) and to develop a formal theory of looting in the S&L industry (e.g., Akerlof and Romer 1993). More recently, the Bernie Madoff scandal has triggered a close review by academics and regulators of the disclosure requirements faced by investment managers. Among other things, such events must cause financial economists to reconsider the degree to which markets or regulations are efficient.

Jay Ritter (2003) discusses recent developments in corporate finance. He identifies two sharp departures from prior paradigms and literature: (1) an increased focus on law and finance, and (2) an increased willingness to accept behavioral factors as determinants of managerial choices, particularly in regard to informational inefficiencies. The reality of market inefficiencies is starkly exposed in the wake of massive financial scandals.

The effect of recent financial scandals and the development of theory, according to Ritter, is likely to be significant. Ritter observes:

The stock market bubble of the late 1990s, in my opinion, is the financial economics equivalent of the Great Depression to macroeconomics—an outlier event so huge, and so difficult to explain within the context of the framework that explains investor behavior most of the time, that it will affect future empirical studies dramatically. (2003, 2)

Finally, one may argue that many financial scandals encourage financial economists to reexamine even well-accepted assumptions and theories. For example, the assumption that "rational expectations" police the market and protect investors against informational asymmetries is clearly weakened by repeated occurrences of massive financial scandals. Principal-agent models that employ compensation schemes, such as performance-based compensation plans, may be well designed consistent with theory but result in perverse and unintended consequences in practice. Financial scandals also invariably produce calls for regulation, such as the Sarbanes-Oxley Act, which change the economic environment and influence the development of financial research.

2.1.4   Investor Activism

Finally, ethics has drawn the attention of financial economists through an increased level of activism among investors concerned about corporate social responsibility, most evident in the large-scale and growing capital flows toward investment funds that identify themselves as investing in stocks of companies that are "socially responsible." Between 1995 and 2005, the total amount of socially screened investments in the United States grew from $635 billion to more than $2.3 trillion, nearly one out of every ten dollars under professional management in the United States. During this period, these socially responsible investment assets increased at a rate 4% higher than the entire managed investments universe in the United States.[2]

It is worth noting that this scale of capital flows cannot be easily explained by accepted capital market theories, since, in brief, restricting the investment universe, as such screened portfolios do, should lead to inefficient portfolios. Such phenomena have motivated many financial economists to study the performance of such funds. (See, e.g., Rivoli 1995.)

2.2   EVIDENCE OF ACADEMIC INTEREST IN FINANCIAL ETHICS

There is some evidence that finance academics are interested in the connections between ethics and finance in teaching, practice, and research. For example, the "Forum on Financial Ethics," organized in 1993 under the auspices of the journal *Financial Management* by editor James Ang, addressed the basic question, what is meant by financial ethics?

In an attempt to flesh out the meaning of financial ethics, Ang's forum also considered the following questions: What are specific examples of ethical or unethical behavior as applied to finance? Is it a real concern to practicing financial managers? and Do finance professors have a responsibility to address questions of ethics in the teaching of finance?[3]

In addition to financial management, other practitioner-oriented finance journals such as The Journal of Applied Corporate Finance, The Journal of Banking and Finance, *The Journal of Portfolio Management, The Financial Analysts Journal,*

---

2. The Social Investment Forum, "2005 Report on Socially Responsible Investment Investing Trends in theUnited States."pg iv.
3. Note that these questions are for the most part normative financial economics. The forum contributors were James S. Ang, W. Scott Bauman, Kit Bingham, Sir Adrian Cadbury, John Dobson, Stephen E. Loeb, Robert D. Rosenbaum, Robert G. Ruland, Hersh Shifrin, and Meir Statman.

and the Journal of Applied Finance (formerly Financial Practice and Education) have published, with more or less frequency, articles that address the ethical dimensions of financial education and practice (e.g., Chami, Cosimano, and Fullenkamp 2002; Dobson 1999, 1993; Cloninger 1997, 1995; Brennan 1994; Jensen 1994; Brickley, Smith, and Zimmerman 1994; Markowitz 1992; Smith 1992; Shefrin and Statman 1993; Cornell and Shapiro 1987; Rudd 1981).

In addition, of course, scores of articles addressing the interactions between ethics and finance have been published in refereed nonfinance journals in the field of business ethics—notably in *The Journal of Business Ethics* and the *Business Ethics Quarterly*—though the contributors have been mainly nonfinance academics. Contributions of particular relevance to finance include Bøhren 1998; Pava and Krausz 1996; Rivoli 1995; Raines and Leathers 1994a; Lee and McKenzie 1994; Davidson and Worrell 1994; Tamari 1990; Kaen, Kaufman, and Zacharias 1988; and Horrigan 1987. Nonetheless, most finance-related articles in business ethics journals have taken a discernible negative view of financial practice.[4] Not surprisingly, perhaps, finance academics have been reluctant to incorporate such materials in their curricula.

Book-length treatments of the relationship between finance and ethics have also appeared, including, notably, Boatright 1999; Dobson 1997; Hoffman, Kamm, Frederick, and Petry 1996; Argandoña 1995; Prindl and Prodhan 1994; Bear and Maldonado-Bear 1994; Bowie and Freeman 1992; and Williams, Reilly, and Houck 1989.

---

4. For example, Boatright and Peterson (2003) observe that business ethics as an academic discipline owes its existence to financial scandals. And in his succinct historical overview of the development of business ethics, De George (1987) argues that the emphasis of business ethics has been largely negative in its attitude toward business practice, focusing on the abuses by business, on lying, false reports, disasters, bribes, and payoffs.

Ethical considerations in finance textbooks have also made some progress. As a benchmark of this trend Hawley (1991) noted that only eleven out of twenty-two popular introductory finance textbooks referenced "ethics," "business ethics," or "social responsibility" in their indexes, and that the maximum coverage was 2.5 pages, almost exclusively confined to the introductory chapter. Yet in contrast, Ivo Welch's corporate finance textbook contains an extensive supplementary chapter discussing the ethical dimension of many financial decisions.[5]

Despite the many worthy contributions noted, the careful reader may have already observed that they seem to have had their heyday in the 1990s. This does raise the obvious questions: Has progress in the development of financial ethics stalled, if not stopped altogether? And if so, why? Before we address these questions, we explore factors that help explain why finance academics should be in the connection between finance and ethics.

2.3   CHALLENGES TO THE INTEGRATION OF ETHICS AND FINANCE

As we have already suggested, despite the growing interest in financial ethics among finance academics, relatively few direct contributions have been made by financial researchers. We attribute this lack of progress to several interrelated factors. First, there is a basic conception of finance as positivist and ethics as normative and, consequently, they are fundamentally incompatible. We characterize this view as the "finance is value-free" argument.

Second, financial economists are not trained in moral argumentation and thus are reluctant to engage in it either

5. See Welch 2006.

in scholarly work or in the classroom. A related concern is that with considerable advances in the development of financial theories and empirical tests it is virtually impossible to introduce complex topics such as ethical reasoning into the finance curricula.

Third, there are relatively few incentives to finance academics to engage in financial ethics research. Unlike contributions to mainstream topics in financial research such as corporate finance, contributions to financial ethics are unlikely to be accepted by referees who view such work in a purely normative way. Related to this, the scarcity of contributions from preeminent financial economists has likely reinforced the notion that financial ethics is unworthy of research efforts. This absence is particularly odd considering many contributions to the role of economics and ethics of Nobel laureates, including the relation between altruism and economics (e.g., Gary Becker, Kenneth Arrow, Amartya Sen, Herbert Simon), the effect of dishonesty in the market (e.g., George Akerlof), the viability of moral rules (such as cooperation) in the large group settings of perfect competition (e.g., James Buchanan), and the role of fairness as a constraint on profit maximization (e.g., Daniel Kahneman). Sen has been particularly prominent in the effort to join modern economics and ethics (see, e.g., Sen 1987). Buchanan (1992) has proposed that an "economic theory of ethics" should take its place alongside the "economic theory of law" and the "economic theory of politics."

2.4   THE FINANCE IS VALUE-FREE ARGUMENT

Perhaps the most commonly accepted view of finance and, for that matter, economics is that these disciplines are value-free. In economics, of course, this has a particularly long legacy given that it developed out of moral philosophy and struggled to become a distinct social science freed from the moral constraints of its origins.

A recent statement of this view by financial economist Clifford Smith is indicative:

> Like other sciences, good economics is "value-free." This does not mean economists do not share the values of their society, only that the primary aim of economics is to describe and predict human behavior, not prescribe it. Such predictions of behavior can then be used to design more effective public or corporate policies. (1992, 23)

While the statement quoted above is fully in the spirit of positivist theory, as we hope to show later, it is also paradoxical. For one thing, it is inescapably normative and judgmental, and thus self-contradictory. Besides imposing a value judgment as to what constitutes "good" economics (and, by implication, what does not), the statement posits a normative goal (teleological end) for the discipline (i.e., the primary aim is to describe and predict) justified by its social and private value as a guide for the design of "more effective public or corporate policies." Moreover, the statement assigns to ethics only a normative dimension (not surprisingly, since this is the way most people probably think of ethics). In its normative character, ethics would then be incompatible with positive theory. The question arises, then, whether ethics can be framed in positivist terms. In other words, whether there is such a thing as "positive ethics"? We answer this question in the affirmative, based on the following reasoning: positive financial ethics involves the use of positivist methodology to examine the economic consequences of ethical concepts and behaviors. Moreover, while the definitions of positivist methodology vary (e.g., Hausman 1989), we adopt the conventional view that positivist economic methodology strives to describe, explain, or predict economic phenomena. The role of positive financial ethics is to describe, explain, or predict economic phenomena from the perspective of moral concepts and ethical expectations. We will discuss this in more detail later, but for now we simply propose that the common view of financial ethics (i.e., that it is purely normative) is incomplete and a barrier to understanding the effects of ethical expectations on economic value.

2.5 FRAMEWORK FOR FINANCIAL ETHICS

Ethical concepts such as honesty, fairness, truth telling, promise keeping, cooperation, and altruism have also recently entered mainstream financial economics research in more explicit form. For example, Jensen (2006) argues that companies with poor governance systems encourage lying and financial manipulation that have been severe enough to destroy the true values of companies, and that these effects need to be discussed in boardrooms and classrooms. Oliver Hart (2001) examines whether the existence of norms such as honesty and trust affect the boundaries of the firm. Herschel Grossman and Minseong Kim (2002a) explore the conditions under which a moral disposition is rewarded, in the sense of moral people being more prosperous than amoral people. Rafael La Porta, Florencio Lopez-De-Silanes, Andrei Shleifer, and Robert Vishny (1997a) test the relationship between trust and economic performance in large organizations. Robert Cooter and Melvin Eisenberg (2000) examine the relationship between fairness and character and economic efficiency of the firm.

Douglas Stevens and Alex Thevaranjan (2002) and Øyvind Bøhren (1998) incorporate an ethically sensitive agent into the classic principal-agent model. Adair Morse and Sophie Shive (2004) and Lauren Cohen (2006) examine the effects of patriotism and loyalty on investment decisions. Bruce Carlin,

Florin Dorobantu, and S.Viswanathan (2009) study a theoretical model of the effects of trust on economic growth.

Thus this approach involves reframing financial ethics from a normative aspect to a positive aspect. For example, whether it is "good" or "bad" for agents to shirk is a normative question, but predicting the economic consequences of shirking is a positive question. Financial economists are not comfortable with the former question but are comfortable with the latter one. Likewise, the economic consequences of lying, dishonesty, fairness, altruism, cooperation, and trustworthiness can be discussed fully within the context of mainstream financial-economic research.

Jensen (2006) attempts to integrate the concept of integrity into finance theory and practice.[6] Acknowledging that finance scholars resist discussions of integrity as being "normative," he emphasizes a scientific role for the concept by relating it to value creation. This, he hopes, will facilitate introducing the language of integrity into the discussions of finance scholars and practitioners.

Emphasizing its instrumental role, he argues that integrity is no more normative than the proposition that using the net present value rule will lead to value creation. Thus he emphasizes the concept of integrity in a positivist sense, rejecting any interpretation of integrity as dealing with morals, ethics, religion, or values. However, this is a very fine distinction since, according to Jensen, a system is in integrity

> when it is whole, complete and stable. That means nothing is hidden, no deception, no untruths, no violation of contracts or property rights, etc. (2006, 5)

---

6. This discussion is based on Jensen's presentation at the American Finance Association annual meeting in 2006. See Jensen, Murphy, and Wruck 2004 and Jensen 2003.

In addition, if one is going to violate "the rules of the game," according to Jensen, integrity requires that one disclose this to all others. Integrity also requires that economic agents fulfill commitments and promises, and, if unable to do so, acknowledge their failures and attempt remedies for any losses resulting from their failures.

To illustrate situations that weaken integrity, Jensen points to several fairly pervasive settings. First, he notes that finance scholars weaken integrity when they too narrowly define fiduciary duty as the duty to current shareholders only, to the exclusion of the interests of future shareholders and bondholders. For example, finance academics typically endorse the sale of overvalued stock or the acquisition (via shares) of companies whose stock is less overvalued than their own. The consequences of these transactions for future stockholders is ignored, and Jensen suggests that this is a violation of integrity and does not serve the long-run interest of shareholders. He poses the rhetorical question, how will the new stockholders react when they realize they have been taken?

Second, firms that use budgets and targets for planning and managerial compensation purposes produce important counterproductive consequences by encouraging gaming the system and impairing value creation. Jensen argues that such compensation systems violate integrity by encouraging lying:

> Almost every company in the world uses a budget or target-setting system that rewards people for ignoring or destroying valuable information and punishes them for taking actions that benefit the company. These budget-based systems reward people for lying, and for lying about their lying, and punish them for telling the truth. These systems reward gaming while obfuscating the facts they are meant to summon: facts that are necessary to help managers make the necessary trade-offs in allocating resources between projects, departments and initiatives. (2003, 380)

Jensen concludes that the impairment of integrity in such compensation-based budgets and targeting systems is so severe that they ought to be discontinued altogether for purposes of compensation.

Jensen (2006) also takes finance scholars to task for condoning managerial practices such as "earnings management" and "income smoothing" without acknowledging that these practices are tantamount to lying. Accordingly, many finance academics who accept this proposition conclude that any ethical dimension to finance research or pedagogy is unwarranted. Indeed, many financial economists consider the "E word" and all its manifestations, that is, honesty, trust, altruism, and fairness impermissible in serious financial research, while others treat it with outright hostility.

2.6   CONCLUSION

From the perspective of positive financial ethics, many "finance" problems are fundamentally "ethics" problems. Thus many economic phenomena such as monitoring, bonding, certification, signaling, incentive contracts, and governance structures can be explained as mechanisms for controlling moral risks. This ethics–centered approach to understanding economic phenomena is similar in spirit to other frameworks that have been applied in positive financial research. Thus the "nexus of contracts" paradigm employed by Jensen and Meckling (1976) in agency theory provides a framework for understanding corporate governance mechanisms as devices for mitigating agency costs and "moral hazards" in contractual relationships. Likewise, the transaction cost "governance structure" framework advanced by, notably, Williamson, provides an alternative lens for explaining the existence of hierarchies relative to markets when opportunistic behavior is assumed. Finally, the roles of reputation and corporate culture in making credible commitments of trust in exchange are employed by David Kreps (1990) to define the purpose of corporations. These various frameworks are not mutually exclusive but rather, mutually enriching ways to deepen our understanding of the same economic phenomena.

CHAPTER 3

Elements of a Positive Financial Ethics

3.1 ETHICAL EXPECTATIONS AND ECONOMIC VALUE

Under uncertainty economic value is determined by expectations. For example, the value of a share of stock reflects the timing, magnitude, and certainty of expected future cash flows. Thus to the extent ethics influences economic value, it must be via expectations. To illustrate, consider a situation in which an outside investor considers the purchase of a share of stock from the corporation. If the outside investor expects to be exploited by insiders, the outside investor will reduce expected cash flows by the amount of the expected exploitation. And the stock price of companies whose executive management is expected to engage in financial manipulation will, all else equal, be less valuable than that of comparable companies (e.g., same systematic risk) whose executive management is expected to be trustworthy.

Once the punitive discount of value is imposed for anticipated unethical behavior, the expected rate of return to the shareholder, in equilibrium, will be the same for both companies, good and bad; that is, it will be determined by the firm's systematic risk only.

Naturally, ethical expectations are formed at least in part by past ethical experience. In addition, the incorporation of various formal and informal safeguards such as contracts, laws, and social norms influence ethical expectations in the market. Of course, these safeguards are not costless. Therefore, even the attempt to improve ethical expectations will not avoid the problem of reducing cash flows.

In the most general sense then, the fundamental proposition of positive financial ethics (PFE) is that the mutual ethical expectations of transacting parties affect the prices of goods and services in exchange. More specifically, ethical expectations introduce, to some extent or another, ethical risk. Ethical risk, in turn, is incorporated in exchange value. As with other positive propositions, this statement is subject to empirical testing. This requires a formulation of the mechanism by which ethical expectations affect value, and a development of objective measures of ethical risk for purposes of empirically testing the effect of expectations on value.

3.2   ETHICAL RISK

We define ethical risk as the expected expropriation of one economic agent by another. By "expropriation" we mean the unwilling or unwitting transfer of value from one party to another; thus expropriation is theft or, since in many cases it is legal, "theft-like." Other synonyms used by financial economists for this type of activity include "predation," "free-riding," "market power," "rent seeking," "implicit compensation," "tunneling," "shirking," "externalities," and "sharking."

All of these activities transgress accepted moral principles such as treating others with dignity, granting others the freedom to decide whether to engage in transactions, honoring trust, and treating others fairly. Thus expropriation is unethical.

While expropriation is unethical, in a narrow economic sense it may represent nothing more than a wealth reallocation between agents with no significant effect on economic efficiency. Dan Usher, for example, argues:

> There is really nothing wrong with theft if one considers the act all by itself. The thief is better off by the amount of money he takes, I am correspondingly worse off, but the national income is not reduced; the thief can be thought of using the money to buy what I would have bought instead. (1987, 236)

Accordingly, as with other redistributions of wealth, and consistent with the second welfare theorem of economics, Pareto optimality is not impaired. That is, following the redistribution, a new Pareto equilibrium results. Moreover, it may be argued that theft economizes on transactions costs and, in that respect, may be efficiency enhancing.

Yet the economic problem with expropriation is not the expropriation itself but its effect on the expectation of theft. This effect not only enters the immediate pending transaction between agents but also creates important social costs and market inefficiencies.

The prospect of expropriation alters behavior among individuals in several respects. For example, potential victims adopt safeguards to minimize or eliminate expropriation risk from predators. One way potential victims protect themselves, at the extreme, is simply to avoid participation in the market altogether; thereby impairing the market process (e.g., Akerlof 1970).

More typically, economically rational agents discount the ex ante value of exchange by the amount of the expected expropriation. Thus in the context of agency cost theory, if a share of stock has an intrinsic value of V and if the capitalized, expected expropriation by insiders is Z, then the rational outside investor will offer V' = V–Z; where V' can be viewed as the exchange value. Thus Z drives a wedge between intrinsic value and market value.

Beyond this, of course, potential victims may call for government intervention to limit the opportunities for expropriation or to enforce moral conduct. While there is an abundance of evidence of government intervention, a dramatic recent example was the passage of the Sarbanes–Oxley Act following the scandals with Enron, WorldCom, and other companies.

Potential predators also create social costs by investing time and effort in devising ways to create new expropriation opportunities rather than engaging in economically productive activity (Usher 1987; Grossman and Kim 2002b).

Ethical risk can be viewed as a product of at least three distinct factors: (1) the dollar magnitude of the potential expropriation, (C); (2) the likelihood of success by the expropriator (q); and (3) the probability that counterparties will in fact behave unethically (P) when given the opportunity. The expected expropriation, Z, is therefore expressed as:

$$Z = P\star q\star C \tag{1}$$

We will argue that expropriation opportunities, that is, $C\star q > 0$ can be characterized as "market failures" since they are generated by informational or other deficiencies (such as market power). Analogously, since exploiting expropriation opportunities reflects a violation of some ethical rule, $P > 0$ can be characterized as "moral failure." Together, market failure and moral failure compose ethical risk. For our purposes, we will assume C and q to be fixed so that we can focus on the role of ethics P.

3.3   ETHICAL RISK AND PERFECT COMPETITION

In financial economic models, ethical expectations enter in two polar forms depending upon the level of market perfection assumed, particularly in regard to information. Theoretically defined, perfect competition assumes that there is no moral failure, thereby eliminating expropriation risk. In our framework, this can be seen directly by setting $P = 0$ in Eq (1). For example, Frank H. Knight argues that, among the conditions necessary for perfect competition,

> We formally exclude all preying of individuals upon each other. There must be no way of acquiring goods except through production and free exchange in the open market. This specification is really a corollary from [other assumptions] which exclude fraud or deceit and theft or brigandage respectively, but it deserves this mention. (1921, 78)

We emphasize the importance of implicit assumptions relating to perfect information in a world of perfect competition. For example, perfect information includes, at least implicitly, instantaneous transparency as to the quality of goods in exchange and the behavior of agents. Since there are no gains to fully revealed deception or other unethical behavior, $P = 0$ whether economic agents are intrinsically immoral or not and thence $Z = 0$ also. In short, there is no ethical risk in the perfect competition model and hence no role for ethical expectations in the narrow, exchange sense we are considering. Moral failure requires departures from the assumptions of the theoretical model detailed by Knight.

3.4   ETHICAL RISK AND IMPERFECT COMPETITION

Opportunities for expropriation require two important departures from the assumptions of the perfect competition model.

For example, when the perfect information assumption is violated, information asymmetries and nontransparency of agent behavior create opportunities for expropriation by increasing q*C, and self-interested agents are assumed to exploit such opportunities. Hence the implicit ethical expectation is that all agents are, at best, amoral (take whatever ethical or unethical action maximizes profits) and thus the probability of exploitation is equal to 1.

In his critique of the perfect competition paradigm Joseph Stiglitz argues that imperfections in information lead to economic behaviors not anticipated by classical theory:

> With perfect information, individuals are paid to perform a particular service; if they perform it they receive the contracted for amount; if they do not, they do not. With imperfect information, firms have to motivate and monitor, rewarding them for observed good performance and punishing them for bad. (2001, 481)

Expected expropriation requires both market failure and moral failure. In the absence of moral failure (i.e., $P = 0$), the classical model holds and there is no chance of expropriation. On the other hand, if $P = 1$, then expropriation opportunities are always fully exploited, and the contemporary finance models hold. The assumption of agents pursuing narrow self-interest implies that $P = 1$. In the next section we further illustrate this point using the Kreps Trust Game.

3.5 POSITIVE FINANCIAL ETHICS: AN ILLUSTRATION FROM GAME THEORY

The connection between the moral concept of trust and economic exchange can be illustrated with Kreps's (1990) example of the "trust game."

This simple example incorporates the two polar assumptions about ethical expectations and the widely different

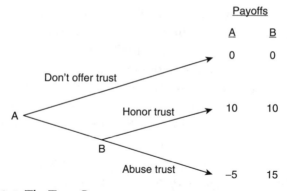

FIGURE 3.1 The Trust Game.

economic consequences. Given the perfect market assumption A extends trust to B and B honors it (i.e., P = 0), resulting in the creation of maximum total value ($20). Yet that is not the result predicted by the contemporary analysis of this game. If this is a one-time transaction, B will rationally abuse trust (i.e., P = 1), and rationally anticipating this, A will not extend trust and the transaction will not take place. Again, this is driven by an ethical expectation (i.e., maximal opportunism) held by A toward B.[1]

1. More abstractly, assume that if A extends trust and B honors it, the payoff to A is y" > y (for simplicity, let y = 0, i.e., the no transaction case), while if A extends trust to B and it is abused, the payoff to A is y'. Clearly, for any y' > 0, A will rationally extend trust even if certain that B will abuse it. In addition, trust may be extended if there is sufficient probability that it will be honored by B even if he is a total stranger.

    We can designate a value, r = y" − y which represents the (marginal) economic rent A expects to earn from the transaction if B honors trust. Thus the expropriation by B is equal to Z = y" − y'. Here we can see that Z affects the distribution of the rent rather than the creation of the rent. In economic terms one may say that efficiency is not impaired by the prospect of expropriation. Shortly, we will argue that A may rationally extend trust even if y' = 0. But notice that in the simple game above we have y' < y = 0, meaning that Z > r (i.e., the expropriation exceeds the marginal rent). In other words, A is not only risking the marginal value but the existing value as well. Stated yet another way,

Since the transaction may be mutually beneficial, Kreps argues that both parties may devise enforcing mechanisms to guarantee that trust will be honored. For example, the parties may negotiate an enforceable contract that will insure A against abuse from B. This will not always work, since contracts may be too costly to enforce and hard to verify. Alternatively, B may provide collateral as insurance that it will honor trust. However, once B has provided the collateral to A, A now has an incentive to abscond with the collateral. In other words, B is forced to trust A and the problem of trust is not resolved.

Generalizing away from the one-shot setting, multiple repetitions of the trust game may generate self-enforcing trust in which the longer-term gains from trust behavior dominate the myopic gains available in the one-shot setting. For example, consider the one-shot arrangement repeated an indefinite number of times. If B honors trust in the first play, the relationship continues, while if B abuses trust in the first play the relationship terminates. Thus over the two plays B receives 20 by honoring trust but only 15 from abusing the trust in the first play. However, it is important to recognize that if A and B know that there are only two plays to the game, A will rationally expect B to defect in the second round and hence will not extend trust in the second round. Conversely, B realizes this and the two-stage game devolves into a one-stage game. And consequently, as in the one-stage game, A expects B to abuse trust in the first round and thus will not extend trust. Thus in order for trust and cooperation to be sustained, neither A nor B must know when it will end (i.e., the game is repeated indefinitely or terminated by a purely random act).

A is entrusting B not only with the marginal product, r, but also with some proportion of his existing wealth.

While the repeated game setting we have described applies to continuing parties, A and B, trust may arise even when the two parties do not maintain a continuing relationship. For example, B may develop a reputation for honoring trust that is conveyed to, for example, potential trustors C through Z. In developing such a reputation, party B is required to pass up at least some opportunities for exploiting trust. Therefore, a reputation for honoring trust is an investment.

3.6   HOW VARIATION IN ETHICAL EXPECTATIONS MAY AFFECT THE TRUST GAME

In the preceding discussion, it was assumed that individuals are either perfectly honest or perfectly dishonest and consequently value creation is achieved or not achieved, respectively. If we now introduce some variation in ethical expectations, a large number of other results are implied. For example, if B can raise A's ethical opinion of him both may gain. In another example, if A is risk neutral and expects to be victimized less than two-thirds of the time in this example she would rationally extend trust (the expected payoff would be at least $2/3(-5) + 1/3(10) = 0$). Thus variations in ethical expectations are reflected in variations in economic values. This cause-and-effect relationship driven by ethical expectations creates important incentives and opportunities to raise them.

There are several good reasons for believing that agent B will not necessarily abuse trust (i.e., $P < 1$) and that this behavior very likely depends upon the diversity among agents and the contexts in which they transact. We cite several reasons why this might be so. First, the implied assumption in contemporary theory as applied to the one-period transaction arrangement is that agents are assumed to be anonymous strangers. However, we argue that the transacting agents might share common social norms. In this case, A has reasonable expectation that to some extent agent B will exhibit shared norms. Conversely, if strangers share nothing, transactions are not undertaken and the absence of such transactions is not observed.

Second, survey data provide some empirical support for this. La Porta et al. (1997a) use data from the World Values Survey in their examination of the relationship between trust and economic performance. In the survey, the trust variable is measured by the percentage of respondents who answered that most people can be trusted when asked "Generally speaking, would you say that most people can be trusted or that you can't be too careful in dealing with people?" A consequence is that trust is neither 0 nor 1, but somewhere in between. It is this variability that is crucial to our model.

For purposes of positive financial ethics, the propensity to abuse trust (P) reflects a priori assessments about the degree to which counterparties will behave in ways *consistent with* moral precepts (i.e., "as-if" they were honest, trustworthy, loyal, fair, and altruistic regardless of their "true" unobservable motivation). Thus there is a distinction between expected observable action and intrinsic ethical character. While these two are unquestionably related, it is the expected quality of action, P, that is of paramount importance to PFE.

Expropriation opportunities, to some extent, naturally induce agents to abuse trust ($P > 0$); that is, "everyone has his price" and thus ethical risk may arise. Counteracting the moral temptation of expropriation opportunities are other considerations by the agent including personal moral values, risk of exposure, punishment, violation of self-esteem, reputation, and other incentive mechanisms. Thus in our framework, P varies from context to context among economic agents.

As noted above, P cannot be observed directly with the exception of, possibly, a direct survey of attitudes. Typically, however, P must be inferred by measures such as the existence of protections and guarantees against expropriation. These "counter-acting" institutions (Akerlof 1970) mitigate ethical risk. Though costly, these institutions enhance exchange value by decreasing the likelihood of expropriation, Douglass North argues:

> Institutions are the humanly devised constraints that structure political, economic and social interaction. They consist of both informal constraints (sanctions, taboos, customs, traditions, and codes of conduct), and formal rules (constitutions, laws, property rights). Throughout history, institutions have been devised by human beings to create order and reduce uncertainty in exchange. Together with the standard constraints of economics they define the choice set and therefore determine transaction and production costs and hence the profitability and feasibility of engaging in economic activity. (1991, 97)

If we introduce a technology cost to reduce expropriation, then we would then use the technology until marginal benefits equal marginal costs. With regard to financial activity, the role of such institutions can be characterized as "financial ethical technologies." They are financial technologies because they add economic value; and they are ethical technologies because their value-enhancing contributions are produced by (explicitly or implicitly) coercing, guaranteeing, or otherwise inducing ethical or, importantly, ethics-like behavior.

3.6.1   Group Size

Another reason to believe that P may be different from 0 and 1 is presented by James Buchanan (1965), who suggests that an agent's likely ethical conduct and, correspondingly, the agent's ethical expectations of others are importantly influenced by the size of the group in which the individual finds himself. In a large group context, Buchanan argues, an individual's "moral" behavior is undermined because individual economic agents behave as if their individual actions have no effect on the ethical actions of others. In contrast, individuals acting in small groups may be able to influence the behavior of others within the groups, either through the process of reciprocity or banishment. As a result, the size of the relevant group may influence individual moral behavior.

External inducements, such as monetary incentives, to act ethically or the existence of punitive mechanisms for unethical actions may also lower P, and thereby increase economic value. Externally induced ethical action may be characterized as "instrumental" or as "ethics-like" behavior. Thus an agent may be said to be "ethical" if he behaves in an "ethics-like" fashion notwithstanding the realism of this assumption.

Consider, for example, the following simple illustration. Two customers enter an expensive jewelry store. One of the customers, T, is a thief whose only objective is to steal something of value in that store. The other customer, H, is perfectly honest and is only interested in examining items for possible purchase. Assume that there is only one clerk in the store and that the clerk believes that one or both of the customers may intend to steal. Without safeguards in place, the clerk will observe the customers very closely in an attempt to discover what their real motivations are, that is, whether they are thieves or honest customers.

Now assume that all the valuable items are securely locked away and that there are surveillance cameras conspicuously placed throughout the store. Finally, assume that these facts are immediately apparent to both customers. Rationally, the thief will not reveal himself and, moreover, the safeguards make the internal ethical motivations of the customers irrelevant to the clerk. However, of course, the safeguards are costly and these costs will be reflected in the price of merchandise. Moreover, the degree to which the store owner invests in safeguards will be influenced by the general level of theft in the area. Thus the investment in safeguards and the consequent price of merchandise are both determined by ethical expectations.

3.6.2   Intrinsic Motivations

Ethicists may and do quarrel over whether "ethical behavior" motivated simply by material gain is truly "ethical." For some, motivations are all-important to the assessment of what constitutes ethical behavior. Thus if an agent is honest purely because honesty is profitable (a "means to an end") rather than out of an intrinsic desire to be honest (an "end in itself") the action may be viewed as purely instrumental and not morally principled. Indeed, such instrumentally ethical individuals may act dishonestly, for example, if it is more profitable to be "dishonest" than honest. In this sense, such individuals may be better characterized as "amoral."

For other ethicists (and financial economists) consequences rather than motivations are all-important. In this sense, agents may be said to act honestly, for example, if their behavior is consistent with that of a truly honest person (the "ethical archetype"). An example of this interpretation is reflected in the so-called "Prudent Man Rule" standard for fiduciary trustees; namely, such trustees are deemed to have made prudent decisions if those decisions reflect what a "Prudent Man" would have done in similar circumstances.

Yet intrinsic motivations are important to PFE, as we will discuss in more detail later. Arguably, the higher the intrinsic moral disposition of agents, the less expensive (more efficient) it will be to induce agents to behave in ways consistent with moral precepts. In this sense, intrinsic moral disposition represents an agent's ethical capital, reflected in the degree to which the agent's intrinsic moral disposition approximates its ethical archetype.

3.7   CONCLUSION

We define ethical risk as the expected expropriation of one agent by another, and show that ethical risk affects economic value through the channel of expectations about ethical behavior. We also decompose ethical risk into the sum of the expected amount that can be expropriated by an agent (market failure) and the likelihood that an agent will indeed expropriate this amount (moral failure). In contrast to neo-classical and contemporary economic theories, we argue that moral failure is not always certain. The degree of moral failure can also vary across agents, depending on several factors, such as the degree of industry competitiveness, whether the participating agents share common social norms, and agents' intrinsic moral dispositions. In the following chapter we discuss further the role of these "financial ethical technologies" in mitigating ethical risk.

CHAPTER 4

The Ethical Technologies of Finance

4.1 INTRODUCTION

Ethical technologies are mechanisms that generate ethical and/or, importantly, ethics-like behavior. These mechanisms are pervasive in financial and economic contexts and are crucial to an understanding of economic phenomena as diverse as capital market regulations, contracts, firms, financial securities, reputation, and even apparently "irrational" economic behavior such as fairness and cooperation in strategic games in the absence of enforcement. This chapter examines ethical technologies particularly relevant to finance.

4.2 FINANCIAL ETHICAL TECHNOLOGIES

Ethical technologies encompass a broad variety of mechanisms that motivate ethical (or, importantly, ethics-like) behavior. Thus they abound in all forms of social interactions including economic, political, and social activities. Formal professions such as medicine and law have elaborate codes and certifying procedures as well as self-regulating organizations to enforce ethical conduct in the profession as alternatives to formal regulation. Certain finance-related professions such as accounting and investment management have adopted similar ethical codes. Less formally, the finance profession in general has adopted its own distinctive ethical technologies, some important examples being incentive contracts, organizational architecture, securities design, other bonding and monitoring mechanisms, investments in reputation building, and financial signaling.

Considered broadly, we distinguish three types of technologies that we somewhat arbitrarily label: instrumental, procedural, and "expressive" technologies. This clearly disputable classification scheme is intended for illustration purposes only. As we will discuss later, there is considerable overlap among categories. However, our intent is to highlight differences among the three approaches rather than similarities. Our categorization loosely follows that of Shaun Heap's (1989) taxonomy of alternative modes of economic rationality.[1]

4.3   OVERVIEW OF ETHICAL TECHNOLOGIES

As noted above, ethical technologies represent formal and informal mechanisms that generate "ethical" conduct in market and nonmarket relationships. Thus perhaps a good place to begin the analysis is with the market in its fully idealized

---

1. Heap identifies three major approaches to economic rationality: instrumental rationality (i.e., what we call maximizing behavior), procedural rationality (i.e., behavior consistent with rules, roles, and norms), and expressive rationality (i.e., behavior consistent with the agent's desire to express his identity). According to Heap, procedural and expressive forms of economic rationality are interdependent since the existence of rules, roles, and norms "enables action to become symbolic: the norms constitute a language which individuals can use to make statements about their ideas of what is worthy" (5).

representation of complete and perfect information, frictionless and costless transactions, and atomistic agents. In such markets, competition disciplines behavior; promise keeping, trust, and honesty, for example, are assured since there is no gain from fully revealed guile and opportunism. Thus economic agents, regardless of their true psychological motivations or moral dispositions, must act "as if" they were ethical, and for that reason these psychological motivations or moral dispositions are ignored.

As markets diverge from the competitive ideal, the role of other, more specialized technologies becomes more explicit. *Instrumental ethical technologies* shape economic agents, through the use of incentives and threats, to behave "as if" they were ethical. Some examples of these specialized technologies include formal regulation, contracts and other monitoring and bonding activities, and governance structures such as firms and financial instruments.

Since these instrumental technologies can be prohibitively expensive and thus rule out certain transactions, *procedural ethical technologies* can provide alternative cost-efficient incentives and threats. Some examples of these procedural technologies include adherence to social norms (i.e., unwritten social contracts) of altruism, fairness, honesty, promise keeping, and so on. Kenneth Arrow (1972) has remarked that norms such as altruism are crucial to the development of economies. Thus to some extent, procedural technologies enable ethics-like behavior that otherwise would not be possible.

Since procedural ethical technologies are valuable when instrumental ethical technologies would not be cost-efficient, procedural technologies help explain behavior (such as fairness in strategic games) even when there is no apparent enforcement incentive or threat. Thus procedural technologies are reflected in what might be revealed in "behavioral" finance or, simply, economic "anomalies" (i.e., apparent violations of the predictions or explanations based on the instrumental view, and/or violations of the narrow rationality assumptions themselves).

While procedural technologies can be viewed, mainly, as complementary to instrumental technologies, they may also serve as symbolic mechanisms that are completely outside the market. Thus some economic behaviors, such as absolute loyalty, may be reflected in economic choices yet be entirely unaffected by the rewards and punishments framework of economic analysis because they are motivated by intentions (identity) rather than consequences (i.e., utility).[2] Since expressive technologies relate to economic choices as expressions of identity, they cannot be "subsumed" in maximizing models.

Procedural and expressive ethical behaviors are molded by education, experience, social norms, and other factors. See, for example, George Akerlof 1983, Jon Elster 1989, and Herbert Simon 1993. Together, procedural and expressive technologies represent the agent's internal ethical capital. In combination, all three types of ethical technologies (instrumental, procedural, and expressive) directly and indirectly affect the costs and feasibility of economic transactions. Clearly, it will typically be difficult to determine which of these main motivations drive particular decisions and actions (Bowles 1998). David Kreps (1997), for example, notes that what appear to be intrinsic motivations (i.e., what we call procedural and expressive) for action may actually be due in part to a response to "fuzzy extrinsic" motivators (i.e., instrumental), such as fear of discharge, censure by fellow employees, or even the desire for coworkers' esteem.

2. The mapping of these technologies into standard ethical models is something like this: instrumental ethical technologies are analogous to act utilitarianism, procedural ethical technologies are analogous to rule utilitarianism, expressive ethical technologies are analogous to the Kantian categorical imperative.

4.4   INSTRUMENTAL ETHICAL TECHNOLOGIES

Instrumental ethical technologies tend to be extrinsic, material, and possess the quid pro quo dimensionality of market transactions. The enforcing mechanism in these instruments is based on the conception of the economic agent as a narrowly self-interested utility maximizer. In Michael Jensen and William Meckling's stark characterization, this economic man "is an evaluator and maximizer who has only one want: money income. He or she is a short-run *money maximizer* who does not care for others, rights, morality, love, respect, or honesty" (1994, 10, emphasis in original).

Despite its narrow characterization, this simple model has thrived for several reasons. First, as Adam Smith proposed, given certain conditions, the narrow pursuit of self-interest, guided as if by an invisible hand, leads to the socially optimal allocation of scarce resources. The formalization of this concept is typically attributed to Edgeworth (Collard 1975). David Collard notes that the fascinating aspect of Edgeworth's treatment is that altruistic themes "were integrated into contract and exchange theory *at its inception*" 355, emphasis in original).

Second, the narrow characterization explains many observed economic phenomena such as contracts, regulation, firms, and other governance structures that are missing from classical economic theory (see, e.g., Coase 1937).

Third, it is reinforced by observations of greed, opportunism, and exploitation in the real world as well as the existence of widespread market failures (Akerlof 1970). Harry Markowitz (1992) discusses two important examples of this prevalent in the 1980s. First, with heavy use of "junk bond" instruments, large leveraged buyouts were executed. The use of such large amounts of new debt basically changed the rules of the game for the old debt holders and reduced the value of their claims. In addition, the high leverage constituted a gamble that the debt could be managed. If not, then the suppliers of the new debt were losers. Here an important distinction is made between the institutions (e.g., S&Ls and insurance companies) that purchased the high-yield debt (with knowledge of the risks) and the uninformed depositors, insurance policyholders, and taxpayers who bore the risks of the gamble without their knowledge or consent and without being able to benefit from the rewards. This risk shifting, Markowitz notes, had important moral consequences.

Instrumental ethical technologies are pervasive, including formal regulation (such as antitrust law that attempts to shore up market discipline of ethics-like behavior by preserving market competition; and criminal and civil laws that discourage antisocial behavior through fines and imprisonment and that coerce minimal standards of honesty, fairness, and trustworthiness in economic transactions). Contracts and other monitoring and bonding mechanisms provide both discipline and incentives for counterparties to behave "as if" they were fully revealing about their private information and actions (Jensen and Meckling 1976). In addition, governance structures such as firms and financial instruments play an important role in settings where contracts are necessarily incomplete and where opportunism is possible (Williamson 1975). Collectively, these devices reflect artifactual solutions to the problem that ethical conduct is not self-enforcing. Moreover, since these technologies become more important as markets depart from the ideal, an endogeneity is created between market perfection and the value of instrumental (and other) ethical technologies. Harold Demsetz remarks,

> The analysis of the free enterprise economy as that economic system to which we *should* aspire does impose a predetermined moral framework within which to work, for it implies that the good

society limits the use of legal sanctions, expands the opportunities for choice by individuals, and, therefore, places the responsibility for behaving ethically on its citizens. (1988, 251, emphasis in original)

We suggest that instrumental ethical technologies become valuable when ethical behavior is itself valuable, for example, when markets are not transparent or economic agents are rationally bounded, increasing the need for trust. In some respects, these technologies can be viewed as forms of insurance. In the contracting framework, this "insurance" may come in the form of a "bribe" via incentives and threats; in the framework of simple one-shot prisoner's dilemma games, the "insurance" may come in the form of "non-cooperation" strategy since this insures minimum loss; in the organizational design framework, the "insurance" is reflected in "command systems" and hierarchies. The cost effectiveness of instrumental ethical technologies will likely depend on expectations of the agent's ethical capital and on the transparency of economic transactions. Eugene Fama and Michael Jensen suggest that the altruism of internal agents allows low cost control of agency problems and acts to bond donors and customers against expropriation. They state:

> Strong tastes for an organization's outputs on the part of internal agents and customers—what we call altruism in the case of non-profits—contribute to the survival of any organization. All organizations try to develop such brand loyalty, but the nonprofits are especially successful, perhaps because of the nature of their products. (1983, 344)

Thus in the instrumental view the ethics problem can be viewed as a dual problem of, on the one hand, unobservable quality and actions ("adverse selection" and "moral hazard"), and, on the other hand, unobservable values. The role of instrumental ethical technologies can be highlighted by noting that the mere unobservability of quality and action need not lead to an ethics problem. For example, in agency theory, under conditions of complete reciprocal trust, agency costs disappear: principals trust agents to honestly report their quality and actions, and agents trust principals to reward them fairly (Bøhren 1998). In the context of the prisoner's dilemma game, Ken Binmore (1994) notes that if the players were perfect Kantians they would realize the first best outcome (i.e., cooperate), but it would then cease to be a prisoner's dilemma game. Since it is unrealistic to expect complete trust, it may be cost effective to undertake monitoring and bonding activities (i.e., instrumental ethical technologies) to induce and/or guarantee trust-like behavior. Since these technologies are costly, at some point they will cease to be efficient and thus the so-called "residual loss" in agency theory (Jensen and Meckling 1976) may also be characterized as "ethical loss."

Below, we provide some illustrative examples of these ethical technologies and some related financial research.

Regulation and corporate governance. Laws relating to the fiduciary role in corporate governance both require duty to the owners of the firm but also allow ethical discretion (Clark 1985). Melvin Eisenberg notes that the American Law Institute's principles of corporate governance provide that, "[e]ven if corporate profit and shareholder gain are not thereby enhanced, the corporation, in the conduct of its business ... may take into account ethical considerations that are reasonably regarded as appropriate to the responsible conduct of business" (1998, 2).

Regulation of financial institutions and markets. In the context of financial institutions, Edward Kane (2002a) notes that financial regulations augment social norms and market discipline to constrain the opportunistic behavior of regulatees. Financial regulations are particularly important because of externalities associated with financial institutions' central role in the economic system. To this end, regulations establish minimal standards and procedures for disclosure, truth telling, promise making, and conciliation. These services offer cost-effective benefits in confidence and convenience to regulated firms and to their customers. Nonetheless, because of their regulatory authority and multiple regulatory missions (among which regulators may prioritize), regulators themselves may be tempted to act opportunistically in their own narrow self-interest.

Hersh Shefrin and Meir Statman (1993) suggest that financial market regulations develop as a result of a changing balance between considerations of efficiency and fairness. They identify seven "entitlements" of fairness: (1) freedom from coercion, (2) freedom from misrepresentation, (3) equal information, (4) equal processing power, (5) freedom from impulse, (6) efficient prices, and (7) equal bargaining power. They contend that policymakers employ an efficiency/fairness framework in much the same way as portfolio managers use a mean/variance framework and thus that any configuration of regulations can be described as a point in the multidimensional efficiency/fairness space. Thus when market participants are viewed as excessively greedy, exploitive, and dishonest, market regulations are more likely to be imposed, even at the cost of market efficiency.

Regulation of insider trading provides a good illustration of the efficiency/fairness trade-off. Those in favor of insider trading argue that profits from the activity provide entrepreneurial rewards (Manne 1966) that consequently benefit shareholders, and insider trading profits may effectively reduce the explicit remuneration required to keep talented management. Dennis Carlton and Daniel Fischel (1983) view insider trading rewards as a cost-effective alternative to contract renegotiation.

Arguments in favor of maintaining prohibitions against insider trading typically rely on arguments of "fairness." Since insiders have significant information advantages relative to outsiders (Kane 2003), prohibitions are considered necessary to avoid exploitation of less-witting shareholders. Lawrence Ausubel (1990) and Michael Manove (1989) present models in which outside investors reduce the level of investment in response to the possible appropriation of profits by insiders. Hence Pareto improvements are possible through the governmental prohibition of the practice. In addition, "moral hazard" concerns may increase with insider trading as insiders will have more incentives to manipulate the quality and/or timing of information released to the public. Kane argues that insiders may intentionally mislead outside investors by releasing financial disinformation (e.g., manipulation of financial statements) and that such disinformation "can account for empirical evidence that security returns show weak positive correlation over weekly and monthly horizons and slight negative serial correlation over longer horizons" (2003, 6). Finally, Utpal Bhattacharya and Matthew Spiegel (1991) contend that if insider trading laws do not exist, the market may fail completely as a communication system because the uninformed might not have the confidence to trade with the insider at all.

Regulation and financial innovation. The use of derivatives such as commodity futures and put and call options is not new. Yet J. Patrick Raines and Charles Leathers (1994a) note that until fairly recent times, trading in such derivatives was viewed as a form of gambling and the derivatives themselves were thus unenforceable in courts of law. What made them gambling devices, they note, was that under prevailing legal theory, an option was inescapably a wagering contract because the purchaser could offer no intent other than a desire to profit by a price change. Other examples of ethical legislation (i.e., to protect the public from unfair competitive practices, fraud, deception, and dishonesty) include the Interstate Commerce Act (1887), the Sherman Antitrust Act (1890), the Clayton Act (1914), and the Securities and Exchange Acts of 1933 and 1934.

Contracts. Jensen and Meckling argue that potential agency problems exist in all collaborative efforts and that "the problem of inducing an 'agent' to behave *as if* he were maximizing the 'principal's' welfare is quite general" (1976, 309, emphasis added). This can often be accomplished with properly designed incentive contracts. From the perspective taken in this work, such arrangements can be said to make the agent behave *as if* he were trustworthy and to make the principal behave *as if* he trusted him.

Reputation. Reputation may also play the role of an instrumental technology, particularly when contracts are necessarily incomplete or prohibitively expensive such as in the case of implicit contracts. The importance of a good commercial reputation was certainly recognized by Adam Smith: "a prudent dealer, who is sensible to his real interest, would rather [choose] to lose what he has a right to than give any ground for suspicion." ("Lecture on the Influence of Commerce on Manners," reprinted in Klein [1997, 18]). The sale of a product conveys not only the product itself but may also carry an implicit contract to maintain repair parts or other necessary support for the product (Jensen and Meckling 1976). Bradford Cornell and Alan Shapiro (1987) suggest that an important enforcing mechanism is provided by a firm's reputation for honesty and promise keeping.

Hierarchies. Agency costs (Jensen and Meckling 1976) and transactions costs (Coase 1937; and Williamson 1975) help define the size and boundary of the firm. Ethical expectations enter into each of these types of costs. For example, Oliver Williamson (1975) argues that if promises were self-enforcing, the importance of assigning transactions to markets or hierarchies would be negligible. Kreps (1990) notes that among the factors affecting transaction costs are the mutual perceptions of the transacting parties of the counterparty's opportunism and guile. Thus it may be beneficial to invest in an ethical reputation as a means of reducing transaction costs. According to Kreps, "This gives us a rather pat explanation for what a firm is: an intangible asset carrying a reputation that is beneficial for efficient transactions, conferring that reputation upon whoever currently owns the asset" (94–95).

Self-regulating organizations. Formal regulation of opportunistic behavior may not always be necessary. In a study of the Chicago, Hong Kong, and Sydney futures markets, Neil Gunningham (1991) suggests that private ordering and informal mechanisms of social control are much more effective in curbing abuses than are formal institutional and governmental sanctions. He notes that peer group pressure, fear of being ostracized, the leverage of large institutional clients, the transparency of certain market dealings, and the opportunities this provides for "pay back" between "repeat players" have often been far more important in ordering behavior than the remote and often unenforced rules imposed either by government or the exchanges themselves.

4.5 PROCEDURAL TECHNOLOGIES

In contrast to the narrow focus on the individual, characteristic of instrumental technologies, *procedural* technologies emphasize the importance of rules, roles, and norms in economic behavior. In Herbert Simon's (e.g., 1993) concept of procedural rationality, individuals accede to social norms (i.e., are "docile") in response to their own bounded rationality. Some procedural technologies, such as norms, are public goods that may be effectively characterized as flowing from an unwritten social contract and that contribute to the overall "fitness" of a group. Elster (1989) examines a broad variety of social norms, including norms of cooperation, fairness, reciprocity, and consumption (such as social etiquette and matters of dress); and work (such as being a team player or doing one's share in joint production). Interestingly, Elster argues that many social norms appear to be a waste of resources without any apparent justification. In addition to broadly accepted social norms, explicit codes of conduct may play a valuable role in constraining opportunistic behavior.

Norm-constrained behavior is reflected in Milton Friedman's famous article on the social responsibility of business:

> In a free-enterprise, private-property system, a corporate executive is an employee of the owners of the business. He has direct responsibility to his employers. That responsibility is to conduct the business in accordance with their desires, which generally will be to make as much money as possible, while conforming to the basic rules of the society, both those embodied in law and those embodied in ethical custom. (1970, 406)

While often vilified for its narrow statement of social responsibility, it seems almost remarkable that so little attention is given to the strong normative character of this mandate and, in particular, its emphasis on adherence to rules, law, and ethical norms.

Codes of conduct communicate norms and standards of expected behavior within professions and the workplace and thus may be valuable in controlling agency costs. Although a formal "standard of practice" or a code of ethics for corporate finance managers has yet to be developed, other management disciplines, such as accounting and investment management, have done so. For example, most investment professionals are governed by standards of practice. W. Scott Bauman (in Ang

1993) notes that a survey of 1,000 financial analysts in the securities investment profession revealed that 97% were subject to standards of practice adopted by their employer organizations. Bauman also reports that the affiliated management of 71% of the respondents "... had considered standards to be of sufficient importance that they assumed responsibility for setting their own standards of professional practices. (1993, 44)"

James Brickley et al. (1994) suggest that corporate agency costs could be mitigated over time by higher ethical standards and that managerial uncertainty about ethical standards may well be a greater corporate problem than their failure to work hard. The challenges in implementing a move toward higher ethical standards is great. Brickley et al. propose two main approaches: first, accept the set of managerial behavioral preferences as given and design contracts and compensation plans that will direct behavior in an ethical manner (i.e., what we have called instrumental technology); second, employ corporate codes of conduct (i.e., what we have called norm-based procedural technology) and training programs that communicate a real concern for good ethical practice.

Douglas Stevens and Alex Thevaranjan (2002), employing the standard principal-agent model of agency theory, demonstrate that incentive-based employment contracts may be dominated or even unnecessary when agents are ethically sensitive and a standard for effort is introduced in the contract. They argue that merely introducing a standard for effort (i.e., specifying the expected effort level) into the traditional principal-agent framework controls the opportunism of ethically sensitive agents. In their model, this works because an ethically sensitive agent feels a utility loss when he chooses to provide less than the contracted level of effort. Thus they contend that their model helps explain why firms commit considerable resources to recruit ethical employees and emphasize professional ethics in employee training.

Colin Camerer and Richard Thaler (1995) characterize norms as forms of "economic etiquette." In this sense they can be viewed as default behaviors, such as the expectation (unless otherwise warranted) that economic agents will "play by the rules" or carry out the responsibilities attaching to one's position in the world (e.g., one may expect a stockbroker to be honest, an agent to be loyal, a judge to be fair). Importantly, many positions of power, such as corporate president or board trustee, often involve elaborate installation ceremonies, including public oaths of office and high public visibility as bonding devices that coerce initiates to transcend narrow self-interest. As we have already noted, procedural technologies can, to some extent, be viewed as a hybrid of instrumental and expressive technologies. They are instrumental to the extent that there may be material and nonmaterial "rents" associated with, for example, being a member of the board. Yet they may also be viewed as expressive, in the sense that they involve a type of public commitment to fulfill the responsibilities associated with them even at some personal sacrifice. As social mechanisms, procedural and expressive technologies may encourage the production of economic externalities missing from the standard instrumental model.

The enforcement of norms often relies on forms of ostracism and shame. Paul Milgrom et al. cite several such examples including:

> The Mishipora, described in the Hebrew Talmud, according to which those who failed to keep promises were punished by being publicly denounced; the use of the "hue and cry" to identify cheaters in Medieval England; the famed "Scarlet Letter," described in Hawthorne's famous story; and the public stocks and pillories of 17th century New England, which were sometimes used to punish errant local merchants. (1990, 19)

Individuals express some autonomy by deciding which norms they will adhere to ("conformist") and which ones they will reject ("rebel"). The act of choice entails costs and benefits but also reflects the autonomous expression of identity.

Social norms and conventions help explain behavior that appears to be "irrational" (i.e., inconsistent with self-interest). For example, Amartya Sen (1997) argues that adherence to norms may conflict with true preferences and thus "revealed preferences" themselves may be conditional on who is doing the choosing as well as the choice set, and thus violate the basic rationality requirement of preference consistency. As an illustration of menu dependence, Sen assumes that two individuals, A and B, are to share a fruit basket containing one mango and two apples, with A choosing first. Even if A prefers mangoes to apples he might still (presumably, following the norm of etiquette) choose an apple, thereby leaving B a choice of either a mango or an apple. Sen also suggests that A might urge B to make the first choice in the hope that he will respond the same way (i.e., leave A with the choice of either mango or apple). Sen refers to this as "strategic nobility." But if, instead, A is presented a fruit basket with two mangoes and two apples then he will prefer to choose a mango thus revealing his true preference. Sen argues that this is a violation of the consistency principle required in the standard definition of rational choice.

Procedural technologies are also revealed in so-called "economic anomalies" (i.e., behavior by economic agents that is inconsistent with the predictions of instrumental rationality). In a selective review of experimental research on games, Camerer and Thaler conclude that many violations of the instrumental rationality assumption have been convincingly documented. For example, in the simple Ultimatum game, two players are to share a sum of money. The first player ("Proposer") offers some portion of the money to the second player ("Responder"). If the Responder accepts, she gets what was offered, and the Proposer gets the rest. If the Responder rejects the offer, both players get nothing. Camerer and Thaler note that

> if both players are income maximizers, and Proposers know this, then the Proposer should offer a penny (or the smallest unit of currency available), and the Responder should accept. Instead, offers typically average about 30–40 percent of the total, with a 50–50 split often the mode. Offers of less than 20percent are frequently rejected. These facts are not now in question. (1995, 210)

Similarly, in the Dictator game, one of the parties, the Allocator, arbitrarily decides what to offer the other party and keeps the rest. If the Allocator is an income maximizer the optimal offer is zero. However, in experimental settings the offer is often positive.

Camerer and Thaler propose that such anomalous behavior is a manifestation of rule following behavior. People have simply adopted

> rules of behavior they think apply to themselves and others, regardless of the situation. They leave tips in restaurants that they never expect to visit again not because they believe this is really a repeated game but because it would be rude to do otherwise. (218)

Likewise, in the ultimatum game, the responder is primarily reacting to the manners of the first player. The responders are willing to turn down rude offers, even at a cost to themselves. Camerer and Thaler argue that incorporating etiquette into economics is different from the typical assumption that altruism is at work (such as other-regarding preferences). They also note that the perceived norms of fairness, investigated by Daniel Kahneman et al. (1986a) can be thought of as rules of polite business practice.

Social dilemma games are similar to prisoner's dilemma games that involve more than two participants. The structure of such games however is similar to the prisoner's dilemma game in that it is in the best self-interest of each participant to defect rather than to cooperate. As in the prisoner's dilemma games, the optimal strategy is 0% cooperation. Yet extensive experiments, set up as "one-shot" games between strangers, result in significant levels of cooperation, as high as 50% (Stout 2001). Stout argues that these counter-theoretical results provide persuasive evidence that other-regarding preferences such as altruism are widespread. She also notes that it is difficult to exclude the possibility that apparently other-regarding behavior actually is motivated entirely by concern for future consequences in the form of reciprocity or reputational loss. "But whatever the internal mechanism, subjects who cooperate in a social dilemma can be said to 'reveal a preference for' (to act as if they care about) serving others' welfare" (10, 11).

Kahneman et al. (1986b) examine the role of fairness in market transactions and propose that both customers and suppliers demonstrate an active willingness to punish unfairness even at some unnecessary personal cost. For example, in a survey of attitudes, they discovered that two equivalent actions might be viewed very differently in terms of fairness. For example, they posed the following question: assuming zero inflation and abundant supply of labor, would a wage reduction of 7% be viewed as "fair" or "unfair"? Sixty-two percent of the respondents considered the action unfair. Yet when the same group was asked if, given 12% inflation, a wage increase of 5% would be considered "fair" or "unfair," 78% responded that it would be fair. They conclude that judgments of fairness are susceptible to substantial framing effects, and that firms have an incentive to frame the terms of exchanges so as to make them appear "fair."

Matthew Rabin (1993) has proposed a "fairness equilibrium" model in which both altruistic behavior toward others and punishment of others depends on one's beliefs about the motives of others. According to Rabin, the same people who are altruistic to other altruistic people are also motivated to hurt those who hurt them. He cites, as an example, that if an employee has been exceptionally loyal, then a manager may feel some obligation to treat that employee well even when it is not in his self-interest to do so.

4.6 EXPRESSIVE TECHNOLOGIES

As statements of identity, expressive technologies are deeply personal and thus virtually impossible to define. Indeed, they may be characterized, to some extent, as reflecting belief systems such as religion. A key feature of expressive ethical technologies is that they are outside of the market. Behaviors, in this view, are motivated not by outcomes (consequences) but rather by intentions. It may be helpful to illustrate the distinction we intend with the use of two simple examples. Assume that a student in an introductory finance course asks the professor "If I see someone's wallet drop onto the floor should I take it?" From an instrumental perspective, the professor might answer "Well, let's see. You might want to estimate how much you think is in the wallet, the probability of being caught, the punishment if you are caught, the damage to your self-esteem whether you are caught or not, etc." In contrast, an expressive approach would simply respond "Are you a thief?" In this approach economic calculations are simply irrelevant. As a more extreme example, consider the following: "Should I kill my grandmother in order to accelerate my inheritance and thus increase its present value?" Any answer that begins with "Well, let's see..." is clearly unsatisfying. The more basic response is "Are you a murderer?" Once that question is answered the calculations are irrelevant.

While the illustrations are clearly simplistic there are many other examples where one's choice of identity, or in other words, fundamental values, simply preempt mechanical calculations in decision making. For example, a person may rationally delegate decision rights to others or foreclose choices altogether. Thomas Schelling refers to this as "anticipatory self-command" by which

> a person in evident possession of her faculties and knowing what she is talking about will rationally seek to prevent, to compel, or to alter her own later behavior—to restrict her own options in violation of what she knows will be her preference at the time the behavior is to take place. It is not a phenomenon that fits easily into a discipline concerned with rational decision, revealed preference, and optimization over time. (1984, 1)

Although we are using the notion of anticipatory self-command somewhat differently from Schelling, the contrast with instrumental methodology (i.e., benefit-cost analysis) is similar. In Schelling's model, the economic agent is viewed as having two "selves," a present self and a future self, and the preferences maintained by each of these selves can be in conflict. Therefore, through the mechanism of anticipatory self-command, the present self maintains intertemporal coherence (i.e., identity) by precluding the exercise of discretion (acts of choice) by the future self. A common example is a person who wants to quit smoking but recognizes that later he will be in a situation that will tempt him to smoke and that he will, consequently, prefer to smoke than not to smoke. Thus anticipating this, he will find a mechanism, such as avoiding the situation altogether, that will preclude any opportunity to smoke later.

Expressive technologies may also be illustrated in the notion of commitment. For example, Sen (1977) distinguishes between "sympathy" and "commitment." The notion of sympathy reflects other-regarding utility, such as reciprocal altruism, in that one economic agent gains from the welfare of another. In that sense, sympathy is similar to instrumentalism since the economic agent's utility is heightened. In contrast, commitment is expressed when a person chooses an action that he believes will yield a lower level of personal welfare to him than an alternative that is also available to him. Thus commitment drives a wedge between personal choice and personal welfare, a situation inconsistent with the instrumental rational choice model in which choices are presumed to be consistent with personal welfare maximization (i.e., revealed preference).

Important examples of commitment may be found in financial securities markets. For example, "socially responsible" mutual funds provide expressive mechanisms for investors who want to make public statements about what they think is "good" or "bad" corporate conduct, even at the cost of some material benefit. These types of funds provide investors an opportunity to integrate social and environmental concerns into investment decisions. This is of interest because in the standard Markowitz portfolio model the only characteristics of concern to the investor should be risk and return. Standard capital market arguments suggest that by restricting the investment universe, socially responsible funds should be less efficient in terms of risk and return than unrestricted funds. Yet as moral expressions, investors may actually prefer lower return for the same level of risk, contrary to the predictions of the equilibrium model. For example, assume investment "A" has the same level of risk as investment "B" but has higher return. Thus "A" should be preferred to "B." But in the socially responsible context, if the investor learns that "A" earns higher rates of return because it engages in "unfair" labor practices, "B" might be preferred.

4.7 ETHICAL TECHNOLOGIES IN THE CONCEPT OF DISCRIMINATING ALIGNMENT

Since ethical expectations vary in degree among economic agents (e.g., with regard to different ethical sensitivities), economic relationships (e.g., with regard to contractual completeness), and characteristics of particular transactions (e.g., with regard to asset specificity), ethical technologies will likewise vary in application and importance in the sense of "discriminating alignments" as articulated by Williamson (1998) in the context of transaction costs economics.

Evidence of such an alignment can be found in the level of volunteerism and other altruistic expressions in civic groups that could not otherwise survive. Fama and Jensen observe:

> Strong tastes for an organization's outputs on the part of internal agents and customers—what we call altruism in the case of nonprofits—contribute to the survival of any organization. All organizations try to develop such brand loyalty, but the nonprofits are especially successful, perhaps because of the nature of their products. (1983, 344)

Simon (1991) notes the important roles of identification and loyalty in motivating employees. According to Simon,

> A department will be less likely to skimp on quality to cut costs if its members identify with the final product. In particular, identification becomes an important means for removing or reducing those inefficiencies that are labeled by the terms "moral hazard" and "opportunism." (41)

4.8 CONFLICTS AMONG THE ETHICAL TECHNOLOGIES

Finally, and ironically, financial ethical technologies typically induce ethical failures of their own. That is to say, while addressing some ethical challenges they almost invariably create new opportunities and incentives for expropriation and hence the need for even additional technologies. In this sense, the evolution of financial ethical technologies may be viewed as the outcome of a continual dialectical process. For example, governmental intervention to ensure confidence in the financial system or to correct "market failures" may induce "government failures" by motivating regulatees to engage in "rent seeking" (see, e.g., Tullock 1967b, 1998), in order to escape or minimize the effects of regulation, or engage in attempts to bribe regulators, and likewise, regulators will discover new opportunities to profit from corruption (see, e.g., Shleifer and Vishny 1993; and Acemoglu and Verdier 2000).

Moreover, intrinsic motivations to work hard, to be altruistic, or to cooperate may be diminished when external monetary incentives are introduced (Frey and Oberholzer-Gee 1997). This is clearly inconsistent with conventional theory, which treats monetary rewards as purely additive to the utility from altruism. Kreps (1997) suggests that the potential conflict between intrinsic motivation and external incentives may be serious enough to challenge fundamental assumptions of agency theory, since extrinsic incentives may destroy the workers' intrinsic motivation or may perversely formalize the employer-employee relationship. "A worker who previously internalized the employer's welfare is sent signals that the relationship is a market exchange and reacts accordingly, taking fuller advantage of opportunities presented to him" (363).

4.9   CONCLUSION

We have attempted to show that a large body of "mainstream" economics and financial research can be examined from the perspective of ethical technologies. In particular, we have argued that many important research areas have emerged in response to ethical failures in the market. Most of this research falls under the heading of "instrumental ethical technologies." Such technologies rely on rewards and penalties to direct economic agents to act "as if" they are ethical. In addition, what we have called norm-based procedural technologies are useful in explaining ethical behavior in the absence of material incentives. For this reason, procedural technologies may be immensely valuable in facilitating transactions that would otherwise be too costly, particularly in regard to implicit agreements, conflicts of interest, and information asymmetries. Finally, we have attempted to illustrate the role of "expressive" technologies as economic behaviors that are completely outside standard economic models.

CHAPTER 5

Studies on the Incidence of Expropriation

5.1 ETHICAL RISKS AND CAPITAL MARKETS

At a macroeconomic level ethical risks can affect economic development, growth, and capital market efficiency. Such ethical risks typically fall under the headings of "expropriation" risk, "predation," and "rent seeking." Key elements in this determination include not only the strength of legal protections for enforcing contracts and protecting property rights but also the strength of social norms to facilitate interpersonal trust.

5.2 ECONOMIC PERFORMANCE ACROSS COUNTRIES

Stephen Knack and Philip Keefer (1997) examine the association of trust and civic cooperation with the economic performance of countries. That such a relationship may be expected is based on the idea that trust and civic cooperation efficiently reduce transactions and enforcement costs in economic activity. Many important transaction relationships readily benefit from such influences. For example, Knack and Keefer argue:

> Trust-sensitive transactions include those in which goods and services are provided in exchange for future payment, employment contracts in which managers rely on employees to accomplish tasks that are difficult to monitor, and investments and savings decisions that rely on assurances by governments or banks that they will not expropriate these assets. Individuals in higher-trust societies spend less to protect themselves from being exploited in economic transactions. Written contracts are less likely to be needed, and they do not have to specify every possible contingency. Litigation may be less frequent. Individuals in high-trust societies are also likely to divert fewer resources to protecting themselves—through tax payments, bribes, or private security services and equipment—from unlawful (criminal) violations of their property rights. Low trust can also discourage innovation. If entrepreneurs must devote more time to monitoring possible malfeasance by partners, employees, and suppliers, they have less time to devote to innovation in new products or processes. Societies characterized by high levels of trust are also less dependent on formal institutions to enforce agreements. Informal credit markets dependent on strong interpersonal trust can facilitate investment where there is no well-developed formal system of financial intermediation, or where lack of assets limits access to bank credit. Interpersonal trust can also provide an imperfect substitute for government-backed property rights or contract enforcement where governments are unable or unwilling to provide them. (1252–1253)

Employing indicators from the World Values Survey for a sample of twenty-nine market economies over the period from 1980 through 1992 Knack and Keefer find that trust and strong norms of civic cooperation are positively and significantly associated with stronger economic performance. They find that the level of trust in a society and the strength of its civic norms are highly correlated and, while they report results including both variables, they conclude that the trust measure is a better measure of social capital for estimation purposes.

As an index of the level of trust in a society, Knack and Keefer use responses to the following World Values Survey question: "Generally speaking, would you say that most people can be trusted, or that you can't be too careful in dealing with people?" Operationally, the level of trust is the percentage of respondents in each nation replying "most people can be trusted" (after deleting the "don't know" responses). The mean value is 35.8%.[1]

The measure of economic performance is the average annual growth in per capita income over the 1980–1992 period. The indicator for trust exhibits a strong and significant relationship to growth. The coefficient on trust suggests that a ten-percentage-point rise in that variable is associated with an eighty-basis-point increase in growth of per capita income over the period.[2]

---

1. In addition to a measure of trust, Knack and Keefer employ a multivariate measure on civic cooperation. They combine responses to questions in the World Values Survey about whether certain behaviors can be justified always, never, or some of the time. The behaviors in question are: (1) claiming government benefits which you are not entitled to; (2) avoiding a fare on public transport; (3) cheating on taxes if you have the chance; (4) keeping money that you have found; and (5) failing to report damage you've done accidentally to a parked vehicle. The responses were then scaled and summed over the five items to create a civic norm index.
2. Other explanatory variables were also used including per capita income in 1980, the proportion of eligible students enrolled in secondary and primary schools in 1960, per capita income at the beginning of the period, and the price level of investment goods, relative to the United States.

5.2.1   Sovereign Expropriation Risk

At the level of national economies, expropriation risk may come from the political regime. For example, outside international investors are vulnerable to expropriation by the sovereign country through the imposition of capital controls, foreign exchange restrictions, and taxes on repatriation of foreign investments. This can be framed as an empirical proposition: countries with greater expropriation risk will necessarily have to offer higher expected returns to foreign investors than will countries with less expropriation risk. Evidence in support of this proposition can be found in several recent studies.

Ravi Bansal and Magnus Dahlquist (2002) examine observed differences in monthly equity risk premia between twenty-one developed and twenty-five emerging markets over the period 1984 through 2001. They suggest that differences in risk premia are partly due to differences in expropriation risk (what they call sample selectivity) across capital markets. In their study, returns are determined by both systematic risks and selectivity bias (the extra compensation that a given market has to pay to international investors for expropriation risk).

Using the world capital asset pricing model (CAPM) to measure systematic risk and a model of country attributes (e.g., the default risk of the sovereign debt) to measure expropriation risk, Bansal and Dahlquist find that after controlling for expropriation risk, systematic risk can explain the cross-sectional variation of returns across countries. The average systematic risk premium (assuming constant betas) is about 45 basis points per month for both emerging and developed economies.

However, the average expropriation risk premium is about 50 basis points in emerging economies and about 0 in developed countries. Thus expropriation risk explains more than half of the ex-post risk premium for emerging economies and close to zero for developed economies. More specifically, the extra return for expropriation risk across emerging countries is about 6% per annum, while it is about 0 in developed countries.

In addition to sovereign expropriation, investors may be vulnerable to expropriation from firms, depending on, for example, the legal regime in particular countries. There is evidence that economic values are lower, costs of capital are higher, capital markets are thinner, and capital markets are smaller in countries with high expropriation risk relative to countries with lower expropriation risk.

Rafael La Porta et al. (1997a) investigate the relationship between the size and breadth of capital markets and investor legal protections in forty-nine countries that vary in the level of investor protections (measured by both the character of legal rules and quality of law enforcement).

To measure the size and breadth of equity markets, they use an adjusted ratio of aggregate stock market value (held by external investors) relative to GNP in 1994; the number of listed domestic firms scaled by population (in millions for 1994); and the number of IPOs, also scaled by population (in millions for 1995 and 1996). Their estimate of the magnitude of credit markets is the sum of bank debt to the private sector and bond market borrowings relative to GNP.

La Porta et al. (1997a) reason that legal protections provide outside investors (i.e., shareholders and creditors) assurances against expropriation from insiders that affects the cost of external financing and hence the demand for external financing. In other words, an expropriation "premium" is incorporated into the cost of equity and debt funds (i.e., the discount in security value resulting from the level of expected expropriation). The premium is negatively related to the strength of legal protections and positively related to expropriation risk. Thus when legal protections are weak and expropriation risk is high, the cost of funds to corporations is high, which reduces the demand for external financing and hence restricts the size of capital markets. According to La Porta et al.):

> When their rights are better protected by the law, outside investors are willing to pay more for financial assets such as equity and debt. They pay more because they recognize that, with better legal protection, more of the firm's profits would come back to them as interest or dividends as opposed to being expropriated by the entrepreneur who controls the firm. By limiting expropriation, the law raises the price that securities fetch in the marketplace. In turn, this enables more entrepreneurs to finance their investments externally, leading to the expansion of financial markets. (2002, 1147)

In addition, they argue that "civil-law" countries (whose origins are French, German, and Scandinavian but which have been adopted by many other countries such as Belgium, Brazil, and Mexico) appear to have weaker investor protections than "common-law" countries (whose origins are the English common law but which have been adopted by other countries such as the United States, Israel, and Thailand). If so, one might expect civil-law countries to have smaller and narrower capital markets than common-law countries.

Their findings are consistent with this hypothesis: on all measures, civil-law countries (particularly French civil-law countries) have narrower and smaller capital markets than common-law countries. For example, the average ratio of outsider-held stock market to GNP is 21% for French civil-law countries and 60% for common-law countries. Common-law countries have thirty-five listed firms per one million people on average compared to ten for the French civil-law countries. Finally, common-law countries, during the

sample period, averaged 2.2 IPOs per million people compared to 0.2 in civil-law countries.

However, as they note, the deeper question is why civil-law
countries are less hospitable to investors. La Porta et al. do
not provide an explanation for this effect but they speculate
that "it is possible that some broad underlying factor, related
to trust, influences the development of all institutions in a
country, including laws and capital markets" (1997a, 1150).

5.2.2   Trust and Expropriation Risk

It may be argued that expropriation risk is related to the
level of trust in a society. More specifically, trust relationships
are inversely related to expropriation risk. Moreover, there is
an endogeneity between trust and expropriation risk; when
expropriation risk is low trust tends to be high, and when
trust is high (perhaps arising from strong social norms or
small-group contexts) expropriation risk is low.

La Porta et al. (1997a) define trust as a tendency to cooperate, perhaps because it is economically rational (i.e., it is
wealth maximizing), or alternatively, as a manifestation of
social norms that establish minimal expectations of cooperation. Hence, from a social welfare standpoint, a society's
capacity for trust affects its relative economic, political, judi-
cial, and social performance (La Porta et al. 1997a). Thus the
following proposition can be examined: the overall level of
economic performance is positively related with the level of
trust in a society.

La Porta et al. hypothesize that

> trust should be more essential for ensuring cooperation between
> strangers, or people who encounter each other infrequently, than
> for supporting cooperation among people who interact fre-
> quently and repeatedly. (1997a, 333)

Large organizations characterized by relatively infrequent encounters among participants such as governments and corporations may thus require higher levels of trust to secure productive cooperation. In addition, civic groups and other voluntary associations depend heavily on mutual cooperation to achieve the organization's goals.

La Porta et al. (1997a) empirically investigate the effect of trust on the performance of large organizations. Their measure of trust is based on the World Values Survey of 1990–1993 (specifically, the percentage of respondents who answered that most people can be trusted when asked "Generally speaking, would you say that most people can be trusted, or that you can't be too careful in dealing with people?"). Their measures of performance include government efficiency (e.g., the level of corruption, tax compliance, and the efficiency of the judiciary), participation in civic organizations, size of the largest firms relative to GNP, and the performance of a society more generally (e.g., infrastructure quality, infant mortality rate, inflation, and GDP growth). They find that the effects of trust on performance are both statistically significant and quantitatively large on virtually every dimension.

Perhaps more remarkably, they find that the level of trust in a country is inversely related to the percentage of the population belonging to a hierarchical religion (Roman Catholicism, Eastern Orthodoxy, or Islam). They report that on average the percentage of population belonging to a hierarchical religion is 55% and its correlation with trust is −0.61. When the hierarchical religion variable is used as an independent variable to explain organizational performance they find:

> Holding per capita income constant, countries with more dominant hierarchical religions have less efficient judiciaries, greater

corruption, lower-quality bureaucracies, higher rates of tax evasion, lower rates of participation in civil activities and professional
associations, a lower level of importance of large firms in the
economy, inferior infrastructures, and higher inflation. (336–337)

5.3   ETHICAL RISKS AND CORPORATE FINANCE

5.3.1   Expropriation Risk across Countries

La Porta et al. (2000) investigate the relationship between
expropriation risk and dividend policies adopted by firms in
different countries in the context of the principal–agent
model. They present two competing models of this relationship. According to one model, (the "outcome model") dividend policies are affected by the strength of legal protections
for outside investors. If legal protections are strong, shareholders can take actions to disgorge dividends from companies that may otherwise waste cash by investing in poor
projects. However, outside investors will not take such action
if the firm has productive use of retained earnings. Consequently, the dividend payout ratio in countries with strong
legal protections will be positively related to the strength
of legal protections and negatively related with growth
opportunities.

Conversely, in countries with weak legal protections, outside investors are unable to effectively force the company to
pay dividends. Thus the prediction of this model is that
countries with weak legal protections for shareholders will
tend to have lower dividend payouts than countries with
strong legal protections.

In contrast to the outcome model, they examine a competing "substitute model." In this model, in countries with
weak legal environments, dividends serve as a reputation
effect, such that firms in such environments will have higher

dividend payout ratios in order to persuade outside investors that they will not be expropriated. Moreover, since high-growth firms with profitable opportunities are likely to require more external financing, firms in weak-protection countries may actually adopt higher payout ratios in order to maintain reputations.

For analytical purposes, the strength of minority share-holder protection is measured by a combination of the type of legal regime (as noted above, common-law countries are considered to have stronger protections than civil-law countries). In addition, they employ an index of anti-director rights (La Porta et al. 1998) (e.g., whether the particular country is above (high protection) or below the median of this index). The index of anti-director rights includes

> the ease of voting for directors, the possibility of electing direc-
> tors through a cumulative voting mechanism, the existence of a
> grievance mechanism for oppressed minority shareholders, such
> as a class action law-suit, the percentage of votes needed to call an
> extraordinary shareholder meeting, and the existence of preemp-
> tive rights. (La Porta et al. 2000, 10)

The data set includes over four thousand firms from thirty-three countries. Dividend payout ratios are estimated in several ways including the most conventional dividends to earnings ratio for the year 1994. Growth opportunities are proxied by the five-year growth rate in sales from 1989 to 1994.

The authors find consistent support for the outcome model of dividend policy determination; that is, countries with strong legal protections for minority shareholders have higher dividend to earnings ratios than countries with weak legal protections. In addition, they argue that in countries with a strong legal protections for minority shareholders, high-growth firms can persuasively pursue low dividend payout ratios because, due to their legal protections, minority share-holders are willing to wait.

5.3.2   Expropriation Risk across Firms

Within particular countries, whereby all firms are subject to the same broad legal regime, expropriation risk may vary across firms depending on several factors. For example, majority (block) shareholders may exploit minority share-holders. Additionally, a misalignment between voting rights and cash flow rights encourages the controlling group to extract private benefits at the expense of minority share-holders. For example, the use of pyramidal organizations can allow a group to gain voting control with relatively little equity investment.

Roberto Barontini and Giovanni Siciliano (2003) investi-gate whether expropriation risk is reflected in stock returns and market values within the Italian stock market. Theo-retically, to the extent security prices are accurately discounted in anticipation of expropriation risk, one might expect to see variation among firms in terms of market values relative to expropriation risk but not in stock returns.

They examine the stock returns and asset values of all listed Italian stocks for the period 1991 through 2000 using a measure of expropriation risk. To assess expropriation risk on stock returns, the authors employ the four-factor Fama-French-Carhart CAPM. The relationship between firm value and expropriation risk is measured by Tobin's "q," con-trolling for other factors, such as growth opportunities and industrial sector.

Expropriation risk enters their models as a dummy vari-able, taking the value of one when expropriation risk is high or very high. In turn, the expropriation dummy is a product of two other dummy variables, what they call a "power dummy" and an "incentive dummy." The power dummy takes the value of one if the controlling (ultimate owner) shareholder has at least 30% of voting rights and the largest outside shareholder has no more than 10% of voting rights. In 1991, 90% of Italian listed companies fit this description (compared to 65% in 2000). The incentive dummy takes a value of one if the controlling shareholder employs a pyramidal group and/ or the ratio of nonvoting (or limited-voting) shares to outstanding shares is more than 20%. Thus "high expropriation risk" is defined as a combination of the power dummy equal to one and an incentive dummy equal to one. In 1991, the proportion of Italian firms fitting this definition was 39% (25% in 2000).

Barontini and Siciliano find that expropriation risk does not affect stock returns, as predicted, but does have a strong negative impact on firm value as measured by Tobin's "q" (which they compute as the ratio between market value of total assets and book value of total assets). The Tobin's "q" ratio for high expropriation firms is 17.5 percentage points lower when the controlling shareholder is a family. They see this value discount as consistent with Michael Jensen and William Meckling's (1976) argument that rational outside investors accurately discount the value of the firm by the amount of the expected expropriation.

Paul Gompers et al. (2001) examine the relationship among corporate governance provisions, firm valuation, and stock-price returns for American firms in the context of takeover activity during the 1990s. In particular, they focus on whether the level of shareholder protections is reflected in firm values and stock rates of return. (They also examine the relationship between corporate governance and operating performance, capital expenditures, and acquisition activity.)

In order to measure corporate governance, they construct a "governance index" made up of twenty-four different pro-management provisions in corporate charters and state takeover laws. Most of these provisions are directly related to management options to resist a hostile takeover, such as poison pills; in almost every case, these provisions give management some tool to resist different types of shareholder activism.

A firm's governance index is increased by one whenever one of the twenty-four provisions applies to the firm. The more protections management has against hostile takeover, the higher the level of the governance index (G), and consequently the more power management has relative to shareholders.

Where corporate governance provisions are weak (i.e., G is high), shareholders anticipate expropriation and rationally discount the value of shares ex ante (Jensen and Meckling 1976). Thus high G firms should have relatively lower market valuations (as measured by Tobin's q) than low G firms. The firms are then grouped into deciles with the top decile representing the "management portfolio" (defined as firms with G equal to or greater than fourteen) and the bottom decile representing the "shareholder portfolio" (defined as firms with G equal to or less than five).

Consistent with theory, Gompers et al. (2001) find that the governance index is highly correlated with firm value. For example, in 1990 the "management portfolio" has an average q ratio of 1.47 compared to 1.77 for the "shareholder portfolio." The difference is statistically significant at the 5% level. Moreover, the relative values diverge consistently over the ten-year period.

As noted, if share prices are properly discounted, subsequent stock-price returns should be determined only by systematic risks (no "abnormal returns"), meaning that relative corporate governance is irrelevant, ex post. By way of illustration, this reasoning underlies the use of "event studies" where, for example, the announcement of a takeover may be reflected in stock prices through abnormal returns around the announcement date but not subsequently. In other words, stock-price returns of companies with weak shareholder protection, all else equal, should not differ from returns from companies with strong shareholder protection given that expropriation risk has already been incorporated in stock prices.

To examine the effect of governance provisions on relative stock returns Gompers et al. (2001) employ the strategy of buying the shareholder portfolio and selling the management portfolio (i.e., zero net investment). The difference in returns is then regressed against the four-factor Fama-French-Carhart CAPM. Surprisingly, the strategy would have earned abnormal returns of 8.5% per year during the ten-year sample period. This result is clearly inconsistent with rational ex ante security valuation. The authors provide several alternative explanations for the result:

> One explanation, suggested by the results of other studies, is that governance provisions that decrease shareholder rights directly cause additional agency costs (e.g., increased CEO pay, decreased leverage, higher capital expenditures and lower productivity at the plant level). If the market underestimates these additional costs, then stock returns would be worse than expected and firm value at the beginning of the period would be too high. The greater agency costs would also show up in lower operating performance. An alternative explanation is that managers understand that future firm performance will be poor, but investors do not foresee this future decline. In this case, prescient managers could put governance provisions in place so as to protect themselves from blame, and while the provisions might have real protective power, they would not necessarily induce additional agency costs. A third explanation is that governance provisions do not themselves have any power, but rather are a signal or symptom of

higher agency costs—a signal not properly incorporated in market prices. (6)

Nonetheless, given the long, ten-year period over which these abnormal returns persist, the failure of investors to adjust more quickly is even harder to explain.

Gompers et al. also find that high-G firms had inferior operating performance, greater capital expenditures, and were more active in making acquisitions than low-G firms. All of these results are consistent with unexpected, higher agency costs of firms with weak corporate governance.

5.4 INTRA-SHAREHOLDER EXPROPRIATION

Shareholder interests are not always homogeneous, and thus the motivation and opportunities for wealth transfers between shareholder groups may arise. For example, "intra-shareholder" transfers may occur between insiders and outside shareholders, and existing shareholders and new shareholders. And there may be cases of controlling shareholders versus minority shareholders, restricted-voting versus superior-voting shareholder classes, and targeted shareholders (i.e., "greenmail") versus nontargeted shareholders. Distinctions are also sometimes made between the interests of "short-term" versus "long-term" investors, and between "institutional" versus "non-institutional" shareholder groups.

5.4.1 "Sharking" and "Tunneling"

Eric Orts (1998) characterizes some forms of wealth expropriation as "sharking." Sharking is the use of authority by principals and quasi-principals (such as large shareholders or corporate management) to redistribute assets to their benefit and at the expense of minority shareholders, creditors, or even rank-and-file employees (e.g., terminating or dramatically altering pension plans).

Simon Johnson et al. (2000) use the term "tunneling" to refer to the transfer of resources out of a company to its controlling shareholder (who is typically also a top manager). They distinguish between two types of tunneling: first, a controlling shareholder can simply transfer resources out of the firm through self-dealing transactions such as outright theft or fraud, asset sales, contracts such as transfer pricing advantageous to the controlling shareholder, excessive executive compensation, loan guarantees, expropriation of corporate opportunities, and so on. Second, the controlling shareholder can exploit various ways to increase voting control at the expense of minority shareholders through, for example, dilutive share issues, minority shareholder freeze-outs, insider trading, acquisitions, or other financial transactions that discriminate against minority shareholders.

While tunneling may be expected in emerging countries where investor legal protections are weak, Johnson et al. examine whether tunneling occurs in developed countries and, if so, whether it is legal. They distinguish between two generic legal regimes: civil-law countries and common-law countries. In addition, they identify two fundamental legal precepts that are adopted by all major countries: the "duty of care" and the "duty of loyalty."

The duty of care requires a director to act in the same manner as a reasonable, prudent, or rational person would act in his position (the "business judgment" rule). The duty of loyalty, or "fiduciary" duty, requires that insiders not profit at the expense of shareholders (the "fairness" rule). Civil-law countries emphasize the duty of care rather than the duty of loyalty while common-law countries place more emphasis on the duty of loyalty. The relative emphasis countries place on these two doctrines appears to influence the degree to which tunneling is accepted.

Johnson et al. describe three types of tunneling: corporate opportunities, transfer pricing, and asset stripping. An example of corporate opportunities tunneling would be a situation in which the controlling shareholder of the firm (possibly also the top executive of the company) might identify a good investment opportunity and, rather than allowing the firm to invest, the controlling shareholder could create a new entity completely owned by the controlling shareholder. The new entity would than pursue the investment opportunity and, thereby, divert value from minority shareholders.

There are an innumerable number of ways in which controlling shareholders may divert corporate opportunities, and their legality might be assessed differently depending upon the legal regime in which they are undertaken, that is, civil law versus common law.

For example, Johnson et al. cite the case of SARL Peronnet, a French company controlled by the Peronnet family. The Peronnet family established a new company, SCI, solely owned by family members. SCI then built a warehouse, which it subsequently leased to SARL Peronnet. The minority shareholders in SARL Peronnet sued the Peronnet family for expropriating the corporate opportunity of SARL Peronnet (namely to build a warehouse), and thereby benefited itself at the expense of minority shareholders.

However, the court ruled in favor of the Peronnet family, on two grounds: first, the arrangement was in the public interest since it allowed the company to expand and, thereby, increase employment; and second, since the warehouse arrangement benefited all SARL Peronnet investors, including the minority investors, by expanding sales, the arrangement had a legitimate business purpose and was not undertaken with the sole intention of benefiting the majority shareholders.

Johnson et al. conclude:

> The court took no interest in the questions of whether the creation of SCI, and the prices it charged SARL Peronnet for the use of the warehouse, were fair to (the minority shareholders). …The court took a very particular interpretation of the effect of the deal on the minority shareholders of SARL Peronnet: as long as they have not suffered an actual loss, the business judgment rule protected the Peronnet family. In the U.S. and the U.K., courts would be very suspicious of the conduct of the Peronnet family unless it could demonstrate that it closely mimicked an arms-length transaction through an independent valuation of the lease and/or approval by independent directors. (2000, 24)

Business groups, in which a controlling shareholder uses pyramids, cross-holdings, or dual-class shares, provide extensive and varied opportunities for tunneling.

Kee-Hong Bae et al. (2002) examine tunneling in the context of mergers and acquisitions by Korean business groups known as chaebols. Chaebols are a group of firms in which ownership is heavily concentrated in one shareholder, typically one family. The family exercises virtually all decision rights and is intimately involved in the management of the chaebol.

For example, within a chaebol one member firm may bid for another member firm. If the controlling family holds a larger position in the target (say 60%) than it does in the acquiring firm (say 20%), there will be incentives to overpay for the acquisition. Overpayment of $1 will benefit the family $.60 from the target at a cost of only $.20 from its ownership of the acquiring firm. Noncontrol shareholders in the bidder thus lose $.80 on the $1 overpayment.

Bae et al. find that when a good-performing chaebol-affiliated firm makes an acquisition of another firm affiliated with the group, it experiences significant negative abnormal returns on the announcement; yet on average, the value of the business group increases because the acquisition enhances the value of other firms in the group. They view this as evidence of tunneling within the business group.

In the absence of expropriation, unanticipated gains and losses are shared proportionally among all shareholders. Thus expropriation may be measured by the difference between the actual benefits or losses to one shareholder group, such as the controlling shareholder, and the proportional benefits or losses that would be predicted given ownership stakes. Mara Faccio and David Stolin (2003) examine unanticipated gains and losses as reflected in abnormal returns from 184 acquisitions by European business groups in the period 1997 to 2000. They first estimate the cumulative four-day abnormal return for the announcement interval for the bidder and convert these returns to dollar magnitudes by multiplying the abnormal return times the preannouncement market value of the bidder.

For example, assume that company B ("bidder"), with a market value of $100 million, announces an acquisition and experiences a negative 10% cumulative abnormal return. The estimated dollar loss for company B would thus be $10 million. If the controlling family in the business group indirectly owns (via pyramidal structures or cross-ownership) 10% of company B, then it should experience a proportional loss of $1 million. This proportional expected loss can then be compared against the actual change in value of the controlling firm.

However, Faccio and Stolin find negative cumulative abnormal returns to the bidding firm and that the net losses to the controlling family across all firms within the business group exceeds the proportional share from the acquisition announcement, though insignificantly so.

They conclude that this result is clearly inconsistent with expropriation. They attribute their results to the likelihood that potential expropriations via acquisitions were already anticipated by minority shareholders and thus incorporated in the initial purchase price of shares and/or that fears of tunneling via acquisitions are overstated.

5.4.2   Multiple Share Classes

In a study of price effects of dual-class shares (restricted voting, RV, versus superior voting, SV), Vijay Jog and Allan Riding (1986) examined 130 stocks traded on the Toronto Stock Exchange, which had introduced a dual class of shares during the period 1976 through 1984. Using event-study methodology, they found a decline in the values of both shares but a larger decline in the RV shares than the SV shares. They caution that there are clear potential abuses in dual-class shares.

In a related study, Ronald Lease, John McConnell, and Wayne Mikkelson (1984) examined the market value of control in six firms with two classes of common stock that differed solely in respect to voting rights. On average, the voting shares traded at a premium relative to the nonvoting shares. They speculate that one possibility could be the expectation that voting shareholders may be able to expropriate the firm's resources at the expense of the nonvoting class. For example, a firm may purchase inputs from (or sell outputs to) another firm owned by controlling stockholders at below (or above) competitive prices.

M. Megan Partch (1987) finds a contrary result in an examination of the effect of the creation of limited voting common stock on the wealth of current stockholders. She studied a sample of forty-four NYSE firms with two classes of voting rights created between 1962 and 1984. She found that shareholder wealth does not appear to be affected by the creation of a class of limited-voting common stock.

Finally, in a study of dual-class ownership in Sweden, Clas Bergström and Kristian Rydqvist (1990) find that controlling shareholders hold proportions of equity larger than needed for control. In so doing, this provides something of a guarantee to the low-vote shares against expropriation by the controlling shareholder, since the controlling shareholder will also be negatively affected by decisions he makes that are detrimental to the firm.

5.4.3   "Greenmail"

Another potential intra-shareholder wealth expropriation method involves anti-takeover maneuvers in which the firm makes targeted repurchases of shares from potential raiders. Typically, though not always, such repurchases are arranged at premium prices not available to other shareholders in the firm. Some of these repurchase transactions, or, "greenmail," have been especially sensational.

James Ang and Alan Tucker (1988) note that Victor Posner's investment of $12.5 million in National Gypsum Co. stock was repurchased for $21.8 million two years later. Irwin Jacobs's investment of $28.3 million in Kaiser Steel Co. stock was repurchased for $61.4 million ten months later.

The share price reactions of greenmail payments are typically negative, suggesting that nontargeted shareholders subsidize the payment of greenmail. Michael Bradley and L. Macdonald Wakeman (1983) report a three-day average abnormal return of −5.5 %. Larry Dann and Harry DeAngelo (1983) find a two-day average abnormal return of −1.8%.

However, this may not be the complete picture since other studies note that at the time of the original buy-in by the potential acquirer, significant positive abnormal returns are generated for nontarget shareholders. Studies that have looked at the combined returns to nontarget shareholders (i.e., the gains from the buy-in less the loss from the greenmail) report positive abnormal net returns.

Clifford Holderness and Dennis Sheehan (1985) report an average positive abnormal return of 3.2% for the combined effects while Wayne Mikkelson and Richard Ruback (1985) report an average net abnormal return of 1.5%. Ang and Tucker (1988) find that target firms exhibit significantly positive abnormal returns of 1.8% for the (buy-in, repurchase) interval.

5.4.4   Insider Trading

Lisa Meulbroeck (1992) examined 184 stocks in which individuals were charged with insider trading by the SEC during the 1980–1989 period. She found that most cases involved small amounts (under $20,000 in profit per security) and minor penalties. Almost 80% of the insider trading episodes were associated with takeovers, mergers, leveraged buyouts, restructuring, and major share acquisitions.

She also found that the price run-up during the insider trading days was about half the size of the price rise on the day the inside information was released, leading her to conclude that insider trading improved the accuracy of stock prices (i.e., incorporated valuable private information).

5.5   EXPROPRIATION FROM OTHER STAKEHOLDERS

Considered as a nexus of contracts, the firm undertakes a multitude of relationships in which opportunities for expropriation may arise. In many cases, these relationships involve implicit contracts between the firm and its non–investor stakeholders, such as its customers, suppliers, providers of complementary services and products, distributors, and employees.

Implicit contracts may not be honored by the firm and its owners when the benefits of such violations exceed their costs (particularly in situations where existing managers are replaced as a result of hostile takeovers).

5.5.1   Expropriation from Employees

The potential for wealth expropriation from employees to shareholders through the violation of implicit contracts has been examined in the context of takeover activity and consequent pension plan terminations in the 1980s. During that time many defined benefit corporate pension plans were significantly overfunded (i.e., the present value of assets exceeded the present value of anticipated retirement liabilities).

One explanation for this overfunding was that the surplus represented an implicit contract between the corporation and employees by which the firm would pay retirees more than legally obliged to (such as through adjustments for cost-of-living increases) in exchange for lower current wage demands as well as efficiencies in recruiting and retaining employees.

By violating this implicit contract (e.g., by terminating the plans and reverting the excess funds to the firm), shareholders could expropriate wealth from employees. Such an action might be particularly attractive in takeover activity since the acquiring firm might feel no obligation to honor the target's implicit contracts.

Thus takeover premia could reflect anticipated wealth expropriations from the termination of overfunded plans with a reversion of the surplus to the bidder.

Tony Tinker and Dimitrios Ghicas (1993) estimate the actual amount of overfunding by using actuarial estimates of actual plans for a sample of takeover and non-takeover firms during the 1980–1985 period. They conclude that both take-overs and pension plan terminations were more frequent the larger the magnitude of the surplus.

Jeffrey Pontiff, Andrei Shleifer, and Michael Weisbach (1990) examine pension plan reversions in the context of both friendly and hostile takeovers during the period 1980–1988. They find that pension plan reversions were twice as likely for hostile takeovers versus friendly takeovers. They suggest that this is consistent with the view that hostile take-overs are more likely to reflect a breach of implicit contracts with employees. They estimate that wealth transfers from pension fund reversions on average represented from 10% to 13% of takeover premia in successful takeovers during the period.

5.5.2   Expropriation from Markets

Wealth expropriations from suppliers and customers by firms are commonly the motives for illegal activities such as fraud, manipulation, and price fixing. When discovered, these ille-gal activities often result in reductions in shareholder wealth that greatly exceed the fines or other punishments imposed on the perpetrator. One way to interpret this evidence is to view the reduction in share value as a reputational penalty. Alternatively, the reduction in share value may simply reflect lowered expectations of the firm's ability to expropriate future wealth as a result of the discovery.

Fraud. Robert Forsythe et al. (1999) examine alternative communication settings relative to the adverse selection problem posed by George Akerlof (1970). In Akerlof's model, there is no communication between buyers and sellers and hence no information about asset quality is exchanged. Yet even if such communication were possible, there is no assurance that it will be truthful and honest. Forsythe et al. examine the efficiency effects of three alternative communication settings: "no communication," "cheap-talk," and an "antifraud rule."

In their experiments, Forsythe et al. define efficiency relative to a full symmetric information outcome in which true quality is known to both buyers and sellers and all products trade. Among other things, they find that when no communication is permitted, results predicted by adverse selection theory are documented; that is, uniformly low adjusted efficiencies (in other words, few trades) are made.

When "cheap-talk" is permitted, sellers are permitted to say anything they wish about the true quality of the product; in other words, they are permitted to lie. Knowing this, rational buyers should discount all such claims to the point where such communication is in effect "no communication." Thus one would expect that the "cheap-talk" trading efficiency would be similar to if not exactly the same as that under the no-communication settings. However, Forsythe et al. find that the "cheap-talk" results are significantly higher in efficiency than predicted by theory. Moreover, the increased efficiency appears to accrue completely to the sellers, indicating a wealth transfer from buyers and sellers. According to Forsythe et al., "The sellers' false claims often deceive buyers, misleading them to purchase many assets at prices above their values" (1999, 498).

Interestingly, they also find that the "antifraud rule" (in which sellers may make any claims they wish about product quality but, among claims they make, they must reveal true product quality. Knowing this, rational buyers should presume that the lowest-quality statement made by the seller is the true quality. Because of this restricted antifraud provision, significantly higher overall efficiencies than the "cheap-talk" setting are produced, and "the increase in efficiency due to imposing the antifraud rule on otherwise unrestricted quality statements accrues completely to the buyers" (1999, 498).

One important implication of their results is that buyers are apparently gullible, and antifraud laws may be effective in improving the efficiency of markets but also in controlling wealth expropriation from buyers to sellers. The evidence of gullibility is inconsistent with rational decision making but what makes their results even more striking is that buyers and sellers randomly alternate in repeated rounds of the experiment, thus sellers who lie about the product quality become gullible buyers when the roles are reversed:

> What makes this result most surprising is that, in our experimental design, subjects alternate between being buyers and sellers. They also meet each other only once in each role and communicate anonymously through a computer network. Thus the buyer's gullibility is not due to a failure to understand the "other" side of the transaction, nor from an attempt at a multiperiod strategy, nor from promised side payments. The same subjects who are quite willing to lie when acting as sellers are quite gullible when acting as buyers. In fact, a subject's dishonesty when acting as a seller correlates positively with the same subject's gullibility when acting as a buyer—apparently a subject who is more likely to make fraudulent statements believes that others are less likely to make such claims. (Forsythe et al. 1999, 483)

Jonathan M. Karpoff and John R. Lott (1993) examine the effects of 132 fraud events for 71 firms during the period 1978–1987. A distinctive aspect of the study is that it focused on cases in which the damaged party did business with the accused firm (e.g., customers, suppliers, employees, and investors); in other words, a stakeholder. They found that alleged or actual corporate fraud announcements caused a significant economic loss to the firm and that only a minor

portion (6.5%) could be attributed to the firm's expected
legal costs and penalties. They suggest that as much as one-
third of the total loss, conservatively, could be attributed to
"lost reputation, that is, the present value of lower output
prices or higher input prices. Furthermore, consistent with
this interpretation, there is some evidence that firms' earnings decline after a fraud announcement. (796)"

Price fixing. Dale Cloninger et al. (1990) estimate the stock
price effects of price fixing. They examine forty-one firms
that were charged with price fixing during the 1950–1970
period. While there are several steps in the prosecution of
price fixing, and thus several event "windows," the authors
found the "indictment" stage to be the most significant, with
a two-day cumulative decline of about 2%.

While the negative stock price reactions are consistent
with related studies that suggest a "reputational" penalty,
the interpretation of the results is unusual. The authors suggest that the results are consistent with the view that managers undertake illegal or unethical business practice on
behalf of shareholders (rather than for their own benefit):
"The presumption that unfair business practices are inconsistent with shareholder interest could be incorrect" (153).
And that it is the expectation that managers will discon-
tinue such behavior in the future that produces the drop in
stock value.

Thus the drop in stock price is not viewed as a penalty
imposed by the stock market on management for past illegal
or unethical business practices, but rather as a penalty for the
discontinuation of such practices. Of course, the consequence of the discovery of illegal activity does fall on shareholders, but it falls on those shareholders who invested in
expectation of the higher profits (generated by the illegal
activity) ignorant of their true nature. In other words, these
shareholders presumably did not know that the firm was

doing anything illegal and hence believed that the firm's level of returns were legitimate.

Jean-Claude Bosch and E. Woodrow Eckard (1991) attempt to explain why firms undertake price fixing and, if it is unprofitable, why a large number persist in it. They estimate that approximately thirteen hundred firms were indicted by the Department of Justice between 1962 and 1980 and that "the proportion of recidivists (as much as 4 times) ... is roughly 14%" (309, fn.1). They note that negative market reactions to price fixing indictments might result from expected legal costs, expected lost monopoly profits, and/or negative market signal effects, such as tarnished reputation.

They examine the market value effects on 127 sample firm observations during the period 1962–1980. In constant 1982 dollars, the total market value losses exceeded $2 billion, of which expected legal costs, including treble damage awards and settlements, "appear to explain only a fraction." (317) They find no effect on the rivals of price fixing firms. While they note that their results are inconclusive, Bosch and Eckard suggest that a significant market value loss to firms guilty of price fixing is due to "expected lost monopoly profits from the conspiracy, rather than lost efficiency or goodwill rents" (317).

Other illegal activities. There is some evidence that stock price reactions to announcements of corporate illegal activities may depend on the type of illegality. Wallace Davidson et al. (1994) examine 535 announcements of alleged illegal corporate activities reported in *The Wall Street Journal* over the twenty-six-year period 1965–1990. They sorted the crimes into ten categories (bribery, tax evasion, theft of trade secrets, financial reporting violations, violations of government contracts, kickbacks, criminal fraud, price fixing, security law violations, and overcharging customers).

For the sample overall, they found no significant stock price reaction. However, they did find significant negative reactions to bribery, tax evasion, theft of trade secrets, financial reporting violations, and violations of government contracts. The other crimes had either insignificant or positive announcement effects.

One puzzling result is that firms cited for price fixing actually had a positive abnormal return on eventday zero. The authors speculate that it may be "that price fixing is so profitable that some shareholders consider it desirable even if the company is caught. Or, it could be a result that occurred by chance" (983).

When only indictment announcements are considered, the positive abnormal returns to price fixing are even larger and more statistically significant on event day zero. Also, interestingly, in comparing ninety-six previously indicted firms in the 1970s, the present study found that forty-nine had again been alleged to have committed crimes in the 1980s. One explanation provided by the authors is that once convicted, firms may be under more scrutiny in the future, hence increasing their probability of being caught again. Alternatively, the authors "cannot reject the notion that the penalties are insufficient." (985)

5.6   CONCLUSION

Even our brief sampling of empirical research into the incidence of expropriation suggests that a broad and vigorous literature exists. Given the overwhelming and increasing volume of research into expropriation, it is clear that the ethical dimension of financial activity is of great importance to financial researchers; it is particularly notable that much of this research is fairly recent. We have attempted to provide a skeletal taxonomy as a way of sorting this research but there is clearly much more than can be done in this regard. Progress in the development of financial ethics will involve not only the elaboration of a richer taxonomy of moral risks but also a parallel analysis of the financial ethical technologies they induce.

CHAPTER 6

Financial Research Relating to Trust

Trust can be defined in a variety of ways. Broadly interpreted, we distinguish between trust behavior, which originates from social norms (what we have previously characterized as norm-based in financial ethical technologies), and trust behavior, which is based on explicit and implicit pecuniary payoffs (what we have previously characterized as instrumental financial ethical technologies). The main distinction we try to draw between these two types of trust behavior is based upon the relative importance of pecuniary incentives to the enforcement of trust. Others make the distinction between "trust" and "trustworthiness" (see, e.g., Hardin 1996); whereby, in our framework, trustworthiness is norm-based while trust is instrumentally enforced.

In the next section, we describe trustworthiness as a moral quality. Following that, we describe trust in its nonmoral (more accurately, quasi-moral) incarnations.

6.1   TRUSTWORTHINESS

Trustworthiness is a moral quality that permits others, that is, trustors, a level of reliance that the trustee will be honest, fair, truthful, or loyal, for example. This level of reliance is influenced by the strength of certain social norms (which convey ex ante expectations) as well as the degree to which the trustor knows the trustworthiness of the trustee, as it might be revealed through frequent contact or reputation. Clearly, this trust may at times be misplaced and the trustor will be victimized by the trustee.

In product and financial market transactions, trust is often related to the expected level of honesty, as in the degree to which exchange partners can rely on the "word" of others. Kenneth Arrow (1968) has remarked that it is useful for individuals to be able to place trust in each other's word as a nonmarket remedy for market failures. Thus when the seller of a good makes claims about its quality and the potential buyer cannot verify the credibility of the claim, trust enters the transaction. If the level of trust is low, the transaction may not take place, even if it would benefit both parties. Arrow notes that trust arises from the internalization of certain social norms thath are viewed as beneficial to economic efficiency and that there is a whole set of customs and norms that might be similarly interpreted as agreements to improve the efficiency of the economic system.

In other situations, the mere extension of trust may inspire nonmaterial motivations in the trustee, such as the desire to "live up" to the moral expectation communicated by the trustor or by inspiring a sense of charity or altruism in the trustee (Pettit 1995). To place one's welfare in the hands of another, willingly and without recourse, reflects an act of faith by the trustor.

A more formal argument is that both the trustor and trustee possess utility functions in which mutual welfare is important. Amartya Sen (1977) and David Collard (1975) note that Edgeworth, while modeling economic man as purely egoistic, nonetheless believed that most agents are in fact partly egoistic and partly altruistic. If so, abusing trust harms both the trustor but also the trustee. This argument is employed by Ralph Chami and Connel Fullenkamp (2001) in their analysis of trust in the principal-agent relationship. They define trust as mutual reciprocal altruism, such that the principal's utility depends on the agent's utility and vice versa. Their model, as described later, permits a first-best solution to agency problems at all levels within the firm.

In economic terms, honoring trust when it is more profitable to abuse trust is not rational. Such events are considered economic anomalies. In the following sections we first discuss game-theoretic models of trust, some mechanized mechanisms for improving corporation, and finally financial research that focuses on the role of trust at the micro- and macroeconomic levels.

6.2   TRUST AND THE PRISONER'S DILEMMA GAME

The role of instrumental technologies in inducing trust behavior even when agents are assumed to be untrustworthy can be illustrated using the Kreps Trust Game described in chapter 3. This game represents a form of the prisoner's dilemma game. In the one-shot form of this game, cooperation cannot succeed, yet when the game is indefinitely repeated, cooperative and trusting behavior may be self-sustaining and enduring.

In the simplest form of this game, two prisoners (A and B) are to be tried for crimes they have committed. The prosecutor

TABLE 6.1   Prisoner's Dilemma Game

		B	
		Don't confess	Confess
A	Don't confess	2,2	20,0
	Confess	0,20	10,10

has solid evidence of a minor crime but weak evidence of the major crime. If both prisoners confess to the major crime, they each receive a sentence of ten years in prison. If neither confesses, they are both sentenced to two years each for the minor crime. If one party confesses but the other does not, the confessor goes free while the non-confessor gets twenty years in prison. The outcome matrix is shown on table 6.1 below with the first number indicating A's sentence, and the second number B's sentence.

As this game is modeled, it is clearly in the best collective interests of the prisoners to cooperate and not confess (each receives a two-year sentence). Yet the optimal strategy for each prisoner is to confess, since regardless of what the other prisoner does, he is always better off.

In the standard analysis of this result, the conclusion is usually drawn that self-interested behavior defeats cooperation and is undesirable from a social perspective. Sen remarks that

> one of the interests in games like the Prisoners' Dilemma lies in the fact that the usual postulates of rational behavior (even after taking into account the preferences of others) yields a situation that is inferior for all. (55)

But something important is missing from this standard conclusion, namely, the relevant specification of "all." The structure of the simple prisoner's dilemma game uses the individualistic impulse of self-interest to produce a socially *desirable* result, that is, criminals confess. Gordon Tullock remarks:

> By deliberately putting the criminals in the dilemma, the prosecutor is acting rationally; and if they follow their individual rationality, society as a whole will be better off than if they behave in a manner which maximizes the payoff of the prisoner's own little two-man society. (1967a, 229)

In many cases, non-cooperation by agents is essential to the efficiency of markets and overall social welfare. There are many instances in which cooperation is not socially desirable. Criminal activity is an example, as are oligopolistic behavior, market manipulation, and so on.

An example where non-cooperation strengthens market competition can be seen in table 6.2 below. Assume a duopoly market with firms A and B. Each firm may choose to sell the common product at either a "high" price or a "low" price. If A chooses a high price and B responds with a low price, A's profits go down and B's profits go up. As in the typical result, A's best response to any of B's possible decisions is to charge a low price (the worst outcome for both), even though both firms would be better off colluding with a high price.

TABLE 6.2   Prisoner's Dilemma Game—High Price vs. Low Price

		B	
		High price	Low price
A	High price	2,2	−2,4
	Low price	4,−2	0,0

Moreover, we argue that the self-interested strategy modeled in the prisoner's dilemma game is driven by each prisoner's *ethical* assessment of the expected behavior of the other: in particular, that the other is not to be trusted, given the structure of incentives. Tullock emphasizes that the game does not involve trust since the optimal behavior of each prisoner is invariant to the actions of the other. As he puts it, "I may have the most perfect confidence that my fellow criminal will never confess without in any way affecting the desirability of my confessing" (229).

However, in the standard form, Prisoner A must rationally assume that Prisoner B will behave in the same way as himself, subject to the same incentives. In other words, A and B are iconically interchangeable and symmetrically rational. If so, one may argue the game is not properly modeled. For example, symmetric rationality is inconsistent with the existence of the following states: (a) Agent A confesses and B doesn't (which implies that B is dumber than A), and (b) Agent A does not confess and B does. The only states consistent with symmetric rationality are that both confess or that neither confesses.

The prisoners are faced with only two symmetrically rational outcomes with decidedly different payoffs for both prisoners. In particular, given our assumptions, mutual silence dominates mutual confession for each.

Consider the following example of a "one-shot" prisoner's dilemma game involving two players, each of which can play one of two pure strategies, "hawk" or "dove." (This discussion and examples are based on Binmore [1994].) For either player, rational self-interest dictates playing "hawk," and thus "hawk, hawk" is the unique Nash equilibrium of the game. Nonetheless, this equilibrium is not Pareto efficient, let alone Pareto optimal, in that both players prefer "dove, dove," since each player would receive $2 instead of $1.

TABLE 6.3   Prisoner's Dilemma Game—Dove vs. Hawk

		B	
		Dove	Hawk
A	Dove	2,2	0,3
	Hawk	3,0	1,1

This obstacle to cooperation is inherent in the modeling of the prisoner's dilemma game. In particular, since neither player knows for certain whether the other player is playing an optimal strategy, "hawk" is superior. For example, if player A plays "hawk" and player B unwittingly plays "dove," player A's payoff is $3; and if player A unwittingly plays "dove" but player B plays "hawk," player A gets $0. Even though player A does not know what strategy player B will use, it makes no difference, since player A's best choice ("hawk") is independent of what player B's choice is.

Ken Binmore addresses the ethical criticism of the dilemma game as being "consequentialist" (i.e., "ends justify means") insofar as the outcomes determine the behavior (i.e., one selects the strategy with the highest payoff). Others, he notes, might argue that some players might select "dove" as a moral (e.g., deontological) act, regardless of the consequences. But he argues that this simply replaces one set of values (e.g., "means justify the ends") for another. Accordingly, as suggested above, two dyed-in-the-wool Kantians might always play "dove, dove" but this would no longer be a prisoner's dilemma game.

In contrast to the one-shot prisoner's dilemma game described above, repeated plays of the game alter the set of equilibrium outcomes since, in essence, the number of possible payoffs increases. In a repeated game, the one-shot prisoner's dilemma is repeated indefinitely until their players' relationship is terminated by a random event. In this case, the payoff (2,2) corresponds to the average per-game payoff from both players repeatedly playing ("dove", "dove"). In contrast, the outcome of (1,2) results from both players playing ("hawk, dove") one-third of the time and ("dove, hawk") two-thirds of the time. This "mixed strategy" requires that both players follow the same strategy (i.e., "hawk, dove" one-third of the time; "dove, hawk" two-thirds). Thus on average, player A gets \$1 = 1/3(3) + 2/3(0) and player B gets \$2 = 1/3(0) + 2/3(3).

Binmore shows that the possible payoffs to the repeated game can be represented geometrically as shown in the figure below.

The coordinates (0,3), (2,2), (3,0), and (1,1) correspond to the average per-game payoffs to the four possible pure strategies in the one-shot game. This includes the cooperative "dove, dove" strategy described above in which both players earn 2 per game. In addition to the pure-strategy payoffs, the broken lines also enclose these the set of payoffs from all possible mixed strategies. The shaded area represents the set of equilibrium outcomes in the repeated game, including the coordinate (1,2) calculated above.

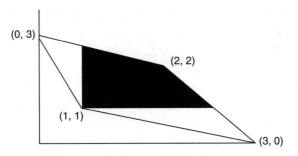

FIGURE 6.1   Equilibria in the Repeated PD Game.

Since both (1,1), which is the strategy of always playing "hawk, hawk," and (2,2), which is the strategy of always playing ("dove, dove"), are included in the solution space, the indefinitely repeated prisoner's dilemma game permits a variety of Pareto improvements (the shaded portion of the line segments [0,3; 3,0]) over the one-shot game.

Binmore's example illustrates how rewards and punishments in a repeated game can produce a cooperative solution in which both players are made better off relative to the one-shot game. He notes that, "It is easy to verify that (2,2) is a Nash equilibrium outcome for the indefinitely repeated Prisoner's Dilemma. Consider the strategy TIT-FOR-TAT. This calls for a player to begin by using 'dove' in the repeated game and then to copy whatever move the opponent made at the previous stage" (Binmore [1994, 116]). If player A tries to cheat by playing "hawk" while player B plays "dove," player B will reciprocate by playing "hawk" on the next play, and every one thereafter, until player A switches back to "dove." In such a case, player A's payoff stream would look like 3, 1, 1, 1 rather than 2, 2, 2, 2.

In repeated games, many other mechanisms, such as "reputation," may influence optimal strategies, in addition to the tit-for-tat rule. Paul Milgrom et. al. have also proposed a model they characterize as "Adjusted Tit-for-Tat," which yields cooperative (i.e., honest play) equilibria in situations where two players may never play against each other again. Their model requires that each player be able to learn the other player's reputation for honest or cooperative behavior. The authors cite several examples in support of this requirement and of their core contention that "institutions sometimes arise to make reputation mechanisms more effective by communicating information (1990, 19)."

Thus in the context of simple, one-shot prisoner's dilemma games, non-cooperative behavior is consistent with rational self-interest and is a dominant strategy even though it is not Pareto efficient. However, as one generalizes away from the simple model to more complex settings involving reciprocity and/or reputation, cooperation may be both rationally self-interested and Pareto optimal. An important consequence of this simple illustration is that the "message" of the game theoretic result (e.g., non-cooperative behavior in one-shot prisoner's dilemma games) may be extremely sensitive to the assumptions employed in modeling the game.

6.3   TRUST AND GROUP SIZE

James Buchanan (1965) suggests that the perfect competition model (i.e., in the "large-group" context) may actually undermine "moral" behavior. This is because individual economic agents behave as if their individual actions have no effect on the ethical actions of others. In other words, agents are ethical "price takers." Yet in small groups, individual agents may be able to influence the behavior of others within the groups. As a result, the size of the relevant group may have consequences for individual moral behavior.

To illustrate Buchanan's argument, we rely on a simplified version of his model. Buchanan considers a situation in which the individual is faced with the decision as to which ethical rule to follow, specifically, whether to follow the moral law (something akin to Kantian morality) or to follow a rule that he calls "the private maxim." He distinguishes the two alternative decision rules as follows:

> By selecting the first (follow the moral law), the individual commits himself to act in subsequent situations on the basis of something like the generalization principle. That is, he will not act in ways other than those which allow his particular action to be

universalized, regardless of the specific consequences. By select-
ing the second rule (the private maxim) instead, he commits
himself in advance to no particular principle of behavior. He
retains full freedom to act on the basis of expedient considerations in each particular instance that arises. (1965, 2)

The individual also assumes that "others" in his relevant
group face the same decision problem, that is, what moral
rule to follow.

Given the choices, there are four possible states, num-
bered 1 through 4 in table 6.4 below. The numbers in each
cell indicate the relative preference the individual has for
each state. For example, the least desirable outcome (1) for
the individual is to follow the moral law when everybody
else practices the rule of private maxim. In such a state, the
individual will be constantly exploited. Outcome (2), follow
the private maxim rule and others also follow the private
maxim, a Hobbesian state of all against all is an "improvement" for the individual over outcome (1) since it reduces
the individual's exploitation. State (3) reflects an idyllic world
in which all agents act morally and thus is an improvement
over (2). Nonetheless, state (4) is the most favorable to the
individual since he

retains complete freedom to follow the dictates of expediency in
particular actions as his own subjective attitudes may suggest, while
also enjoying a wider freedom to act, if he so chooses, strictly in
terms of the categorical imperative. (Buchanan 1965, 3)

As a result of direct experience, observations, and other
information, the individual assigns a probability distribution
to the expected actions of "others" (what we designate as
the variable P in chapter 3). For example, assume that the
individual believes that 40% of "others" (e.g., as shown in
parentheses in table 6.5 below) will follow the moral law

TABLE 6.4   Individual Payoffs to Possible Moral Rules Followed by
Individuals and Others

Individual	Others	
	Follow private maxim	Follow moral law
Follow private maxim	2	4
Follow moral law	1	3

while the remainder, 60% of others, will follow the private maxim. With this information, the expected value of the alternative ethical rules to the individual can be calculated by multiplying the state by the probability of it occurring.

As shown in table 6.5, following the private maxim dominates following the moral law. And hence, the rational individual can be predicted to follow self-serving behavior. More important, Buchanan (1965) remarks that this choice, follow the private maxim, will dominate whenever the relevant group is of "sufficient" size, which is indeterminate except that it is the point at which the behavior of others becomes exogenous to the individual.

TABLE 6.5   Self-Interest and the Large Group Context

Individual	Others		Expected value
	Follow private maxim	Follow moral law	
Follow private maxim	2 (0.6)	4 (0.4)	2.8
Follow moral law	1 (0.6)	3 (0.4)	1.8

In the large-group context, no individual can hope to influence the ethical behavior of others and, as a result, following the private maxim will be the dominant choice regardless of the probabilities assigned to the behavior of others in the large-group context. There are two reasons for this. First, the rank ordering of states is assumed to follow in the fashion described; as long as the relative ordering is maintained, the actual "payoffs" (e.g., monetary rewards) are irrelevant. Second, in a large-group context the probability that others will behave in particular ways (e.g., that is, in this example, up to 40% will follow the moral law) is exogenous. This is indicated in the table by the fact that the proportions of others who are expected to follow the moral law is independent of whatever decision the individual makes as to his own behavior.

However, in a small-group context, the behavior of others is endogenized: each person believes that his actions will affect the actions of others (perhaps through the process of reciprocity or other penalties such as banishment).

For simplicity, assume that if the individual follows the moral law the probability that others will do so is altered (i.e., the probabilities assigned in the bottom row) as indicated in table 6.6 below.

TABLE 6.6 Self-Interest and the Small Group Context

Individual	Others		Expected value
	Follow private maxim	Follow moral law	
Follow private maxim	2 (0.6)	4 (0.4)	2.8
Follow moral law	1 (0.0)	3 (1.0)	3

Thus if the individual knows that by following the moral law, everyone else will (with a probability of 1.0), then the expected value of following the moral law will actually be higher for all. In this particular example, Buchanan is illustrating how, by following the moral law, individuals may raise the ethical expectations held among members of the group, given the small-group context. An important corollary is that by following self-serving behavior, individuals within small groups may also undermine the moral behavior of others.

Since the atomistic competitive model is promoted as an economic ideal, social policy tends to force individuals into the anonymous large-group context. Thus a significant tension arises between the pursuit of economic efficiency, that is, perfect competition, on the one hand, and undermining incentives for ethical behavior, on the other. One alternative is to resort to "moral legislation," which imposes rules and standards of conduct common to all individuals. As Buchanan observes:

> Once the large-number dilemma is understood, the failure of the market process to produce optimal results when public goods are present is explained. Further, as the argument has been developed, an explanation is provided for the tendency of individuals to turn to changes in the rules, specifically to the introduction of political-governmental processes as substitutes for market processes. Such changes in the institutions or rules can, of course, impose upon all members of the group common standards of conduct. From the analysis developed along these lines it becomes conceptually possible to demonstrate why, under certain circumstances, individuals will, on purely rational grounds, agree to allow themselves to be coerced. (1965, 9)

Many common observations support Buchanan's argument that group size influences many types of behavior.

As he notes, volunteer fire departments arise in villages not in metropolitan centers, crime rates increase consistently with city size, there is honor among thieves, and "time-tested honor systems in universities and colleges collapse when enrollments exceed critical size limits." (1965, 8)

6.4   TRUST AND PRINCIPAL-AGENT RELATIONSHIPS

Chami and Fullenkamp (2001) propose that trust may be incorporated within the standard principal/agent analysis (at the "macro" level between owners and managers) and that it may provide Pareto improvements over the standard (i.e., compensation and monitoring) solutions.

In addition, they argue that, unlike standard solutions, trust may play a valuable role in addressing principal/agent types of problems at the "micro" level between supervisors and regular employees as well as among peer employees. At this "micro" level, standard remedies of incentive compensation and monitoring are not feasible. One reason these approaches do not work in the large corporation is that the connection between the typical employee's work efforts and the corporation's stock price is tenuous at best, so that the impact on incentives is minimal.

An alternative approach to the standard agency problem, noted by the authors, is one based on loyalty. Yet they find this approach also lacking in that "it still omits the agency relationship between employees" (4). And they note that "managers have relatively limited influence over employee compensation contracts or other means to purchase loyalty" (4).

A further difficulty with the compensation/loyalty approaches is that they focus on altering the agent's incentives but take the principal's incentives as given. The alternative preferred by the authors is one based on trust, which they define as symmetric altruism, "where the weight on the other person's utility is close to unity" (6).

At the "macro" firm level, the authors focus on three models of the firm: the Leaner and Meaner firm; the Paternalistic firm; and the Trusting firm. In addition, they imply two additional models: a "Nirvana"-type firm characterized by non-opportunistic owners and managers and the Profit Sharing firm in which agents inherit the firm in an intergenerational context. The authors suggest that the Profit Sharing firm has much in common with the Trusting firm (profit sharing and trust become substitutes). Also, the reciprocal altruism incorporated in the model of the Trusting firm has much in common with the non-opportunistic assumptions in the "Nirvana"-type firm.

A first best solution (which some might characterize as the "Nirvana" firm) is suggested where the principal offers a fixed wage (to insure the agent against fluctuations in income) and the agent works as hard as possible to maximize the revenues of the firm. However, this arrangement is infeasible because the worker's effort is unobservable. Hence, firms with this arrangement will go out of business as agents shirk.

Recognizing the moral hazard problem, a more practical solution involves making the agent somewhat responsible for the compensation received. Compared to the "Nirvana" solution, this solution results in both the principal and agent absorbing some deadweight costs in that revenues and wages are not as high as they might be, monitoring costs may be incurred, and the agent is exposed to wage uncertainty (hence the designation "Leaner and Meaner").

Like the "Nirvana" firm, the Paternalistic firm assumes non-opportunistic (more specifically, altruistic) behavior by the principal; but, since the agent is assumed to be opportunistic, the Paternalistic firm is doomed because the altruism is asymmetric.

In contrast to the Leaner and Meaner firm solution, which is well accepted in the economic agency literature, the authors demonstrate that a new alternative, which they characterize as the Trusting Firm, produces Pareto improvements over the Leaner and Meaner firm.

The key feature of the Trusting Firm is that it models trust as symmetric altruism. Thus not only is the principal generous in providing a wage contract that better insures the agent but the agent in turn works hard to insure high revenues for the principal.

There is broad agreement in the economics literature that cooperative behavior, including symmetric altruism, can produce Pareto improvements in situations where moral hazard is present. As we discuss in chapter 4, Herbert Simon (1991) notes the important roles of identification and loyalty in motivating employees. The authors suggest that trust can be cultivated by the firm by ceding some control over the work process to the employees, by carefully screening job applicants, and by swiftly and harshly punishing transgressors.

Control over the work process may be vital to developing trust in certain kinds of tasks and work environments, such as those involving creative activities, but the bulk of employees may face relatively mundane, routine chores. In these less sophisticated activities, employees may not want additional control and the accountability for the work process, necessitating other mechanisms. This raises the practical question as to whether the cultivation of trust should vary within different sectors of the corporation and, if so, is it consistent for a manager, for example, to exhibit altruism toward some employees but not others?

6.5 CONCLUSION

Existing literature shows that trust plays a significant role in product and financial market transactions. In the standard analysis of prisoner's dilemma games, for example, individual self-interest limits the ability of agents to achieve better outcomes through trust and cooperation, especially in one-shot games. In more complex settings, trust can be improved through other factors including reciprocity, group size, and/or reputation, and therefore lead to cooperation among agents. In addition, incorporating trust within the standard agency framework can lead to Pareto improvements over standard solutions to principal/agent problems.

References

Acemoglu, Daron, and Thierry Verdier. 2000. "The choice between market failures and corruption." *American Economic Review* (March): 194–211.

Akerlof, George A. 1970. "The market for 'lemons': Quality uncertainty and the market mechanism." *Quarterly Journal of Economics* (August): 488–500.

———. 1983. "Loyalty filters." *American Economic Review* (March): 54–63.

Akerlof, George A., and Paul M. Romer. 1993 "Looting: The economic underworld of bankruptcy for profit." *Brookings Papers on Economic Activity* 2:1–74.

Ang, James S. 1993. "Forum on financial ethics." *Financial Management* (Autumn): 32–59.

Ang, James S., and Alan L. Tucker. 1988. "The shareholder wealth effects of corporate greenmail." *Journal of Financial Research* (Winter): 265–280.

Argandoña, Antonio, ed. 1995. *The Ethical Dimension of Financial Institutions and Markets.* Berlin: Springer Verlag, 1995.

Arrow, Kenneth J. 1968. "Economics of moral hazard: Further comment." *American Economic Review* (June): 537–539.

———. 1972. "Gifts and exhanges." *Philosophy and Public Affairs* (1972): 343–362.

Ausubel, Lawrence M. 1990. "Insider trading in a rational expectations economy." *American Economic Review* (December): 1022–1041.

Bae, Kee-Hong, Jun-Koo Kang, and Jin-Mo Kim. 2002. "Tunneling or value added? Evidence from mergers by Korean business groups." *Journal of Finance* (December): 2695–2740.

Bansal, Ravi, and Magnus Dahlquist. 2002. "Expropriation risk and return in global equity markets." Working paper, Duke University.

Barontini, Roberto, and Giovanni Siciliano. 2003. "Equity prices and the risk of expropriation: An analysis of the Italian stock market." ECGI-Finance Working Paper 24/2003.

Bear, Larry A., and Rita Maldonado-Bear. 1994. *Free Markets, Finance, Ethics, and Law.* Englewood Cliffs, N.J.: Prentice Hall, 1994.

Becker, Gary S. 1992. "The economic way of looking at life." Nobel Memorial Prize Lecture, presented December 9, 1992, Stockholm. Published in *Prize Lectures in Economic Sciences*: 1991–1995 38–58. Hackensack: World Scientific, 1997.

Bergström, Clas, and Kristian Rydqvist. 1990. "Ownership of equity in dual-class firms." *Journal of Banking and Finance* (August): 255–269.

Bhattacharya, Utpal, and Matthew Spiegel. 1991. "Insiders, outsiders and market breakdowns." *Review of Financial Studies* 2:255–282.

Binmore, Ken. 1994. *Game Theory and the Social Contract, Volume I: Playing Fair.* Cambridge, Mass.: MIT Press.

Boatright, John R. 1999. *Ethics in Finance.* Malden, Mass.: Blackwell.

Boatright, John R., and Jeffrey Peterson. 2003. "Introduction: Special issue on finance." *Business Ethics Quarterly* (July): 265–270.

Bosch, Jean-Claude, and E. Woodrow Eckard. 1991. "The profitability of price-fixing: Evidence from stock market reaction to federal indictments." *Review of Economics and Statistics* (May): 309–317.

Bowie, Norman E., and R. Edward Freeman, eds. 1992. *Ethics and Agency Theory.* New York: Oxford University Press.

Bowles, Samuel. 1998. "Endogenous preferences: The cultural consequences of markets and other economic institutions." *Journal of Economic Literature* (March): 75–111.

Bøhren, Øyvind. 1998. "The agent's ethics in the principal-agent model." *Journal of Business Ethics* (May): 745–755.

Bradley, Michael, and L. Macdonald Wakeman. 1983. "The wealth effects of targeted share repurchases." *Journal of Financial Economics* (1983): 301–328.

Brennan, Michael J. 1995. "Corporate finance over the past twenty-five years." Silver anniversary commemoration, *Financial Management* (Summer): 9–22.

———. 1994. "Incentives, rationality, and society." *Journal of Applied Corporate Finance* (Summer): 31–39.

Brickley, James, Clifford W. Smith, and Jerold L. Zimmerman. 1994.
"Ethics, incentives, and organizational control." *Journal of Applied
Corporate Finance* (Summer): 20–30.

Buchanan, James M. 1992. "Economic science in the future." *Eastern
Economic Journal* (Fall): 401–403.

———. 1965. "Ethical rules, expected values, and large numbers." *Ethics*
(October): 1–13.

Buffet, Warren. 2003. Berkshire Hathaway Inc. 2002 Annual Report. 1–76.

Camerer, Colin, and Richard H. Thaler. 1995. "Anomalies: Ultimatums,
dictators and manners." *Journal of Economic Perspectives* (Spring):
209–219.

Carlin, Bruce I., Florin Dorobantu, and S. Viswanathan. 2009. "Public
trust, the law, and financial investment." *Journal of Financial Economics*
(June): 321–341.

Carlton, Dennis W., and Daniel R. Fischel. 1983. "The regulation of
insider trading." *Stanford Law Review* (May): 857–895.

Chami, Ralph, Thomas F. Cosimano, and Connel Fullenkamp. 2002.
"Managing ethical risk: How investing in ethics adds value." *Journal
of Banking and Finance* (September): 1697–1718.

Chami, Ralph, and Connel Fullenkamp. 2001. "Trust and efficiency."
Working paper, International Monetary Fund. Available at SSRN:
http://ssrn.com/abstract=206368.

Clark, Robert C. 1985. "Agency costs versus fiduciary duties." In
Principals and Agents: The Structure of Business, ed. J. W. Pratt and
R. J. Zeckhauser, 55–80. Boston: Harvard Business School Press.

Cloninger, Dale O. 1995. "Managerial goals and ethical behavior."
Financial Practice & Education (Spring/Summer): 50–59.

———. 1997. "Share price maximization, asymmetric information and
ethical behavior: A comment," *Financial Practice and Education* (Fall/
Winter): 82–84.

Cloninger, Dale O., Terrance R. Skantz, and Thomas H. Strickland.
1990. "Price-fixing and shareholder returns: An empirical study."
Financial Review (February): 153–163.

Coase, Ronald. H. 1937. "The nature of the firm." *Economica*, n.s. 4:
386–405.

Cohen, Lauren. 2006. "Loyalty based portfolio choice." Working paper,
University of Chicago.

Collard, David. 1975. "Edgeworth's propositions on altruism." *The
Economic Journal* (June): 355–360.

Cooter, Robert D., and Melvin Eisenberg. 2000. "Fairness, character, and efficiency in firms." Berkeley Program in Law & Economics Working Paper Series 42.

Cornell, Bradford, and Alan C. Shapiro. 1987. "Corporate stakeholders and corporate finance." *Financial Management* (Spring): 5–14.

Dann, Larry Y., and Harry DeAngelo. 1983. "Standstill agreements, privately negotiated stock repurchases, and the market for corporate control." *Journal of Financial Economics* (April): 275–300.

Davidson, Wallace N., III, Dan L. Worrell, and Chun I. Lee. 1994. "Stock market reactions to announced corporate illegalities." *Journal of Business Ethics* (December): 979–987.

De George, Richard T. 2005. "A history of business ethics." Paper delivered on February 19, 2005 at *The Accountable Corporation*, the third biennial global business ethics conference sponsored by the Markkula Center for Applied Ethics.

———. 1987. "The status of business ethics: Past and future." *Journal of Business Ethics* (April): 201–211.

Demsetz, Harold. 1988. The Organization of Economic Activity. New York: Blackwell.

Dobson, John. 1997. Financial Ethics. Lanham, Md.: Rowman and Littlefield.

———. 1999. "Is shareholder wealth maximization immoral?" *Financial Analysts Journal* (September/October): 69–75.

———. 1993. "The role of ethics in finance." *Financial Analysts Journal* (November/December): 57–61.

Eisenberg, Melvin A. 1998. "Corporate conduct that does not maximize shareholder gain: Legal conduct, ethical conduct, the penumbra effect, reciprocity, the prisoner's dilemma, sheep's clothing, social conduct, and disclosure." *Stetson Law Review* (Summer): 1–27.

Elster, Jon. 1989. "Social norms and economic theory." *Journal of Economic Perspectives* (Autumn): 99–117.

Faccio, Mara, and Stolin, David. 2003. "Expropriation vs. proportional sharing in corporate acquisitions." Working paper, Vanderbilt University. A later version appeared in the *Journal of Business* (May 2006): 1413–1444.

Fama, Eugene F., and Michael C. Jensen. 1983. "Agency problems and residual claims." *Journal of Law and Economics* (June): 327–349.

Forsythe, Robert, Russell Lundholm, and Thomas Rietz. 1999. "Cheap talk, fraud, and adverse selection in financial markets: Some experimental evidence." *Review of Financial Studies* (Autumn): 481–518.

Frey, Bruno S., and Felix Oberholzer-Gee. 1997. "The cost of price incentives: An empirical analysis of motivation crowding-out." *American Economic Review* (September): 746–755.

Friedman, Milton. 1970. "The social responsibility of business is to increase its profits." *The New York Times Magazine* (September 13): 126–131.

Gibbons, Michael R. 1987. "The interrelations of finance and economics: Empirical perspectives." *American Economic Review* (May 1987): 35–41.

Gompers, Paul A., Joy L. Ishii, and Andrew Metrick. 2001. "Corporate governance and equity prices." NBER Working Paper W8449.

Grossman, Herschel I., and Minseong Kim. 2002a. "Is a moral disposition rewarded?" *Journal of Banking and Finance* (September): 1811–1820.

———. 2002b. "Predation, efficiency, and inequality." *Journal of Institutional and Theoretical Economics* (September): 393–407.

Gunningham, Neil. 1991. "Private ordering, self-regulation and futures markets: A comparative study of informal social control." *Law and Policy* (October): 297–326.

Hardin, Russell. 1996. "Trustworthiness." *Ethics* (October): 26–42.

Hart, Oliver. 2001. "Norms and the theory of the firm." Discussion Paper Number 1923, Harvard Institute of Economic Research (May).

Hausman, Daniel M. 1989. "Economic methodology in a nutshell." *Journal of Economic Perspectives* (Spring): 115–127.

Hausman, Daniel M., and Michael S. McPherson. 1993. "Taking ethics seriously: Economics and contemporary moral philosophy." *Journal of Economic Literature* (June): 671–731.

Hawley, Delvin D. 1991. "Business ethics and social responsibility in finance instruction: An abdication of responsibility." *Journal of Business Ethics* (September): 711–721.

Heap, Shaun H. 1989. *Rationality in Economics*. Oxford: Blackwell.

Hirshleifer, Jack. 1985. "The expanding domain of economics." *American Economic Review* (December): 53–68.

Hoffman, Michael W., Judith B. Kamm, Robert E. Frederick, and Edward S. Petry, eds. 1996. *The Ethics of Accounting and Finance.* Westport, Conn.: Quorum.

Holderness, Clifford G., and Dennis P. Sheehan. 1985. "Raiders or saviors: The evidence on six controversial investors," *Journal of Financial Economics* (December): 555–579.

Horrigan, James O. 1987. "The ethics of the new finance." *Journal of Business Ethics* (February): 97–110.

Jensen, Michael C. 2003. "Paying people to lie: The truth about the budgeting process." *European Financial Management* (September): 379–406.

————. 2006. "Putting integrity into finance theory and practice: A positive approach (PDF of keynote slides)." Based on Harvard NOM Research Paper no. 06–06. Available at SSRN, http://ssrn.com/abstract=876312. First presented at the meetings of the American Finance Association, Boston, Mass., January 6.

————. 1994. "Self-interest, altruism, incentives and agency theory." *Journal of Applied Corporate Finance* (Summer): 40–45.

Jensen, Michael C., and William H. Meckling. 1994. "The nature of man." *Journal of Applied Corporate Finance* (Summer): 4–19.

Jensen, Michael C., and William H. Meckling. 1976. "Theory of the firm: Managerial behavior, agency costs and ownership structure." *Journal of Financial Economics* (October): 305–360.

Jensen, Michael C., Kevin J. Murphy, and Eric G. Wruck. 2004. "Remuneration: Where we've been, how we got to here, what are the problems, and how to fix them." ECGI Finance Working Paper 44/2004.

Jog, Vijay M., and Allan L. Riding. 1986. "Price effects of dual-class shares." *Financial Analysts Journal* (January/February): 58–67.

Johnson, Simon, Rafael La Porta, Florencio Lopez-de-Silanes, and Andrei Shleifer. 2000. "Tunneling." *American Economic Review* (May): 22–27.

Kaen, Fred R., Allen Kaufman, and Larry Zacharias. 1988. "American political values and agency theory: A perspective." *Journal of Business Ethics* (November): 805–820.

Kahneman, Daniel, Jack L. Knetsch, and Richard H. Thaler. 1986a. "Fairness and the assumptions of economics." *Journal of Business* (October, part 2): 285–300.

————. 1986b. "Fairness as a constraint of profit seeking: Entitlements in the market." *American Economic Review* (September): 728–741.

Kane, Edward J. 2003. "Continuing dangers of misinformation in corporate accounting reports." Working paper, Boston College.

————. 1990. "Principal-agent problems in S&L salvage." *Journal of Finance* (July): 755–764.

————. 2002a. "Using deferred compensation to strengthen the ethics of financial regulation." *Journal of Banking & Finance* (September): 1919–1933.

————. 2002b. "What economic principles should policymakers in other countries have learned from the S&L mess?" 2002 NABE Adam Smith Award Address, delivered January 25.

Karpoff, Jonathan M. and John R. Lott. 1993. "The reputational penalty firms bear for committing criminal fraud." *Journal of Law & Economics* (October): 757–802.

Klein, Daniel B., ed. 1997. *Reputation: Studies in the Voluntary Elicitation of Good Conduct.* Ann Arbor: University of Michigan Press.

Knack, Stephen, and Philip Keefer. 1997. "Does social capital have an economic payoff? A cross-country investigation." *Quarterly Journal of Economics* (November): 1251–1288.

Knight, Frank H. 1921. *Risk, Uncertainty and Profit.* Boston: Houghton Mifflin.

Konow, James. 2003. "Which is the fairest one of all? A positive analysis of justice theories." *Journal of Economic Literature* (December): 1188–1239.

Kreps, David M. 1990. "Corporate culture and economic theory." In *Perspectives on Positive Political Economy,* ed. James E. Alt and Kenneth A. Shepsle, 90–143. Cambridge: Cambridge University Press.

————. 1997. "Intrinsic motivation and extrinsic incentives." *American Economic Review* (May): 359–364.

La Porta, Rafael, Florencio Lopez-De-Silanes, Andrei Shleifer, and Robert W. Vishny. 2000. "Agency problems and dividend policies around the world." *Journal of Finance* (February): 1–33.

————. 2002. "Investor protection and corporate valuation." *Journal of Finance* (June): 1147–1170.

————. 1998. "Law and Finance." *Journal of Political Economy* (December): 1113–55.

————. 1997a. "Legal determinants of external finance." *Journal of Finance* (July): 1131–1150.

————. 1997b. "Trust in large organizations." *American Economic Review* (May): 333–338.

Lease, Ronald C., John J. McConnell, and Wayne H. Mikkelson. 1984. "The market value of differential voting rights in closely held corporations." *Journal of Business* (October): 443–467.

Lee, Dwight R., and Richard B. McKenzie. 1994. "Corporate failure as a means to corporate responsibility." *Journal of Business Ethics* (December): 969–978.

Manne, Henry G. 1966. "In defense of insider trading." *Harvard Business Review* (November–December): 113–122.

Manove, Michael. 1989. "The harm from insider trading and informed speculation." *Quarterly Journal of Economics* (November): 823–845.

Markowitz, Harry M. 1992. "Markets and morality." *Journal of Portfolio Management* (Winter): 84–93.

Meulbroek, Lisa K. 1992. "An empirical analysis of illegal insider trading." *Journal of Finance* (December): 1661–1699.

Mikkelson, Wayne, and Richard S. Ruback. 1985. "An empirical analysis of the interfirm equity investment process." *Journal of Financial Economics* (December): 523–553.

Milgrom, Paul R., Douglass C. North, and Barry R. Weingast. 1990. "The role of institutions in the revival of trade: The law merchant, private judges, and the champagne fairs." *Economics and Politics* (March): 1–23.

Morse, Adair, and Sophie Shive. 2004. "Patriotism in your portfolio." Working paper, University of Michigan.

North, Douglass C. 1991. "Institutions." *Journal of Economic Perspectives* (Winter): 97–112.

Orts, Eric W 1998. "Shirking and sharking: A legal theory of the firm." *Yale Law and Policy Review* 16, 2:264–329.

Partch, M. Megan. 1987. "The creation of a class of limited voting common stock and shareholder wealth." *Journal of Financial Economics* (June): 313–339.

Pava, Moses L., and Joshua Krausz. 1996. "The association between corporate social-responsibility and financial performance: The paradox of social cost." *Journal of Business Ethics* (March): 321–357.

Pettit, Philip. 1995. "The cunning of trust." *Philosophy and Public Affairs* (Summer): 202–225.

Pontiff, Jeffrey, Andrei Shleifer, and Michael Weisbach. 1990. "Reversions of excess pension assets after takeovers." *Rand Journal of Economics* (Winter): 600–613.

Prindl, Andreas R., and Bimal Prodhan, eds. 1994. *Ethical Conflicts in Finance*. Oxford: Blackwell Finance.

Rabin, Matthew. 1993. "Incorporating fairness into game theory and economics." *American Economic Review* (December): 1281–1302.

Raines, J. Patrick, and Charles G. Leathers. 1994a. "Financial derivative instruments and social ethics." *Journal of Business Ethics* (March): 197–204.

————. 1994b. "The new speculative stock market: Why the weak immunizing effect of the 1987 crash?" *Journal of Economic Issues* (September): 733–753.

Ritter, Jay R. 2003. "Introduction to recent developments in corporate finance." Working paper, University of Florida (October 19). Subsequently published in *Recent Developments in Corporate Finance, Volumes 1 and 2*, ed. Jay R. Ritter. Northampton, Mass.: Edward Elgar (2005).

Rivoli, Pietra. 1995. "Ethical aspects of investor behavior." *Journal of Business Ethics* (April): 265–277.

Rudd, Andrew. 1981. "Social responsibility and portfolio performance." *California Management Review* (Summer): 55–61.

Schelling, Thomas C. 1984. "Self-command in practice, in policy, and in a theory of rational choice." *American Economic Review* (May): 1–11.

Sen, Amartya K. 1996. "Choice, orderings and morality." In *Ethics and Economics: Volume I*, ed. Alan P. Hamlin, 54–67. Northampton, Mass.: Edward Elgar.

————. 1997. "Maximization and the act of choice." *Econometrica* (July): 745–779.

————. 1987. *On Ethics and Economics*. Oxford: Blackwell.

————. 1977. "Rational fools: A critique of the behavioral foundations of economic theory." *Philosophy & Public Affairs* (Summer): 317–344.

Shefrin, Hersh, and Meir Statman. 1993. "Ethics, fairness, and efficiency in financial markets." *Financial Analysts Journal* (November/December): 21–29.

Shleifer, Andrei, and Robert W. Vishny. 1993. "Corruption." *Quarterly Journal of Economics* (August): 599–617.

Simon, Herbert A. 1993. "Altruism and Economics." *American Economic Review* (May): 156–161.

———. 1991. "Organizations and Markets." *Journal of Economic Perspectives* (Spring): 25–44.

Smith, Clifford W., Jr. 1992. "Economics and ethics: The case of Salomon Brothers." *Journal of Applied Corporate Finance* (Summer): 23–28.

Stevens, Douglas E., and Alex Thevaranjan. 2002. "Ethics and Agency Theory: Incorporating a standard for effort and an ethically sensitive agent." Working paper, Syracuse University.

Stiglitz, Joseph E. 2001. "Information and the change in the paradigm in economics." Nobel Memorial Prize Lecture (December 8). In Les Prix Nobel: The Nobel Prizes 2001, ed. Tore Frängsmyr. Stockholm: Nobel Foundation, 2002.

Stout, Lynn A. 2001. "Other-regarding preferences and social norms." Working Paper 265902, Georgetown University Law Center.

Tamari, Meir. 1990. "Ethical issues in bankruptcy: A Jewish perspective." *Journal of Business Ethics* (October): 785–789.

Tinker, Tony, and Dimitrios Ghicas. 1993. "Dishonored contracts: Accounting and the expropriation of employee pension wealth." *Accounting, Organizations, and Society* (May): 361–380.

Tullock, Gordon. 1967a. "The prisoner's dilemma and mutual trust." *Ethics* (April): 229–230.

———. 1967b. "The welfare cost of monopoly tariffs and theft." *Western Economic Journal* (June): 224–232.

———. 1998. "Which rectangle?" *Public Choice* (September): 405–410.

Usher, Dan. 1987. "Theft as a paradigm for departures from efficiency." *Oxford Economic Papers* (June): 235–252.

Welch, Ivo. 2006. "Ethics (Web Chapter)." (January). Available at SSRN http://papers.ssrn.com/sol3/papers.cfm?abstract_id=876124.

Williams, Oliver F., Frank K. Reilly, and John W. Houck, eds. 1989. *Ethics and the Investment Industry.* Savage, Md.: Rowman and Littlefield, 1989.

Williamson, Oliver E. 1998. "The institutions of governance." *American Economic Review* (May): 75–79.

———. 1975. *Markets and Hierarchies: Analysis and Antitrust Implications.* New York: Free.

Index